GETTING DOWN TO BUSIN

Getting Down to Business

A manual for training businesswomen

USCHI KRAUS-HARPER
MALCOLM HARPER

INTERMEDIATE TECHNOLOGY PUBLICATIONS   1992

Intermediate Technology Publications
103/105 Southampton Row, London WC1B 4HH, UK

© IT Publications 1992

ISBN 1 85339 113 1

Typeset by Inforum Typesetting, Portsmouth
Printed in Great Britain by SRP, Exeter

Contents

ACKNOWLEDGEMENTS

WE HAVE BOTH been involved for many years in training enterprising people, and those who finance, advise and themselves train them, and the main source of the ideas in this book has been the people who have submitted themselves to our training, and our colleagues who have worked with us. They, and their institutions, are too numerous to mention here. We are grateful to all of them.

The staff of certain institutions have, however, played a particularly important role in the genesis and development of this manual, and we are happy to acknowledge them by name:

○ The Unit for the Integration of Women into Industrial Development of the United Nations Industrial Development Organization (UNIDO) invited us to contribute to the design and delivery of training for women in food processing businesses in Africa, and this experience initiated the creation of this training material.

○ Colleagues and course participants from the Pan-African Institute for Development in Eastern and Southern Africa, in Kabwe, Zambia, Ranche House College in Harare, Management Systems International of Washington D.C., the Enterprise Development Centre at Cranfield School of Management in England and the Xavier Institute of Management, Bhubaneswar, India, provided invaluable advice and assistance in the writing and field testing of the material.

Since this manual is part of a continuing process of evolution, we should also like to acknowledge in advance the contributions of those readers who, we hope, will modify, add to and improve the material as they use it. Please share your ideas with us; we can be reached at: c/o Cranfield School of Management, Cranfield, Bedford MK43 0AL, England.

Above all, however, we want to thank the enterprising women who have participated in our training courses and have criticized and commented on the material, and the many others who have not benefited, or perhaps suffered, from our training efforts but have inspired us by their own commitment, hard work and persistence. We hope that this manual will make a modest contribution to enabling a few of them to achieve even more for themselves, for their families and for society in general.

USCHI KRAUS-HARPER
MALCOLM HARPER
Bhubaneswar, India
May 1991

Enterprising women

THIS IS A TRAINERS' manual, which is designed to help you, the trainer, to organize and conduct more effective training courses for enterprising women. Before going into the details of which particular women the manual is intended for, and how to select and train them, it is important to set such training in the overall context of the phenomenon of enterprising women.

Some 70 per cent of all informal sector micro enterprises worldwide are run by women. This means that millions of women are generating income through one or more, mainly micro-business, activities. Some of these activities develop into formal small, sometimes medium and, very rarely, large businesses. Other more wealthy women start small businesses in the formal sector. Some of these businesses, too, develop into successful big companies.

Who are they?

Who are these millions of women, what do they do, what pulls and pushes them to generate income through self-employment or business instead of getting safe jobs or staying at home and being 'proper' wives and mothers?

Most of them belong to the poorer, often the very poorest, strata of society. They may have been to school for a few years, but most of them are illiterate; two-thirds of the world's illiterates are women; female illiteracy rates in some countries are as high as 90 per cent. Also, more and more middle class women are to be found among the enterprising women. An increasing number of women earn the main or even the only income of the household; they are the heads of their households, in legal terms, because there is no one else, or in fact, because their income is the essential one. If it is not the main income, it is, nevertheless, very often not only a minor or occasional contribution but the most regular contribution, the backbone of the family's income, because their husbands are seasonal or casual labourers.

Every country has many such women, but they are often the invisible hands – they keep in the background, running their activities from home. Often their husbands are the formal owners of the business, the ones who apply for, and get, loans and training, while in reality the wives are doing the work, managing the resources. In some countries this is because of discriminatory laws, in others because of local customs; women prefer to stay at home if they can afford to, or it may even be considered improper for women to work outside the house.

When 'experts' talk or write about 'women entrepreneurs' they often mean the few well-educated women who run formal small, medium or large businesses. Their perception, then, is that there are not many businesswomen, that they have to be created. But it is not only the size or status of a business that creates this misconception; it is also that many of the women we have been talking about do not fit into the vague conceptions of what an entrepreneur is; they do not seem to be innovative, they do not seem to take real risks, their activities remain small, there seems to be no urge for expansion, for re-investing profits.

But these women are generating important income, for the family and for society, because they provide what the formal economies of their countries seem to be unable to provide: money to send children to school, money for medical bills, money to increase standards of living, money for survival.

In this manual, therefore, we have tried to avoid the terms 'entrepreneur' or 'entrepreneuse', we use 'enterprising women' for all the women generating any size of income through self-employment and micro-business, and 'successful business women' for those women who, for example, have successfully expanded their activities from self-employment to a small or bigger business employing other people.

What do they do?

If we look at what women *do* – that is, if we look at the woman instead of her business – we realize that women have thousands of ways to generate income. Many if not most of these activities can hardly be called business. The activities may be run from home, they may be seasonal, or casual, they may change frequently, each may create only a tiny income. So it is important to look at the ways women generate income; for low income, self-employed women Usha Jumani (1991) found five types of work/production relationships:

- ○ Wage work
- ○ Piece rate work
- ○ Unpaid family work
- ○ Own account work
- ○ Small entrepreneur

These types of relationships are not only true for low income women; but middle or high income women have greater chances to expand their activities into medium or even large business because, among other reasons, they have easier access to capital and they are more likely to have an effective network of contacts in the business world.

Most of these activities or businesses are taking place in what is called the traditional sector: handicrafts, food-procesing, tailoring, vending and the like. This is one of the reasons why some people do not consider these women to be 'entrepreneurial'. Why is this so? Because women's education, be it formal or informal, is geared towards such traditional activities, and it is here where their skills and strengths *seem* to lie; but it is also because women are less mobile, they have fewer chances to be exposed to new

ideas, and, last but not least, because such activities require less or no initial capital.

The women for whom this manual is intended may have started, or want to start, a business in the traditional or in the non-traditional sector. What is important is that they should want to cross a 'barrier' – for example from piece-rate work for a contractor to own account work, or from own account work to micro-business, employing one to five people, or from micro-business to small business, employing more than five people. And by 'own account work' we do not mean a woman who is apparently self-employed but in reality works for one or even more contractors who provide the raw material and collect the finished goods. This training manual is meant to help women to cross those 'barriers' and thus become more independent, stronger and, we hope, more succesful.

Why do they do it?

A number of studies have been made of the motivation of individuals – into why they start businesses. But most of these studies are based on research about male entrepreneurs. It seems to be a vicious circle: because women's income-generating activities are not seen as businesses, women who do run such activities are not included in research. Research then produces results that are male-biased, leading to an understanding of 'business' and to types of training that are male-biased.

Thus, we do not know much about the motivation of women and tend to put their motivation into 'boxes' such as 'to earn a living', 'to have a hobby', 'to find self-fulfilment'. Our own experience in working with enterprising women shows us that their motivation is far more complex. There is, of course, the basic need for survival which pushes many women into self-employment or micro-business; jobs are scarce, more so for women, especially illiterate women. But why do women go on running all these activities once their basis needs are secured? Because, for example, their financial contribution to the family income may have brought them more respect within the family and society, to the extent that husbands stop beating them; they may have gained more say in family matters, or they have become more 'public' people, enjoying interaction with others through their business activities. It may be that they cannot find a job that provides enough flexibility to enable them to take care of small children, and so on. There are many, many more motives.

You, the trainer, should be aware of the immense variety of needs of your course participants. You should also be totally confident of the great value of running a course for women; such courses are still too often considered to be somewhat marginal and not to be taken seriously. That is wrong. As one Zambian businesswoman put it: 'If you educate a woman, you educate the country.'

Women's income is more likely to be spent for the benefit of their children, their family, than men's income. Women are also known to be more serious in business in that they pay back their loans more reliably than men. In all our studies and experience of enterprise credit we have *never* come across a loan scheme where the male borrowers' repayment record is better than the women's. And women are increasingly recognized, worldwide, as better managers because of their ability to work in a team, motivating other people instead of dominating them.

At the end of this manual you will find a bibliography which includes many books or articles confirming, reinforcing or contradicting what we have said here, and providing a lot of detailed information and case studies about enterprising women.

Should women be trained separately from men?

Every trainer must decide for herself

WE MAY ACCEPT that many social and economic benefits arise from women's businesses, for the reasons outlined in the previous chapter, but this does not in itself mean that women should be trained for self-employment separately from men. There may be good arguments for 'positive discrimination', to ensure that women get a larger share of any assistance that is provided, whether it be in the form of loans, extension services or training courses, but a larger share does not in itself necessarily imply separate provision.

There are, in fact, a number of powerful arguments *against* having separate training courses for women, and anyone who is planning to use the material in this manual should be aware of these, and of the opposing arguments, in order to be able to make the right decision for the particular people for whom she works.

We shall therefore summarize some of the arguments on both sides of this difficult and contentious issue, so that every reader can decide for herself. The session guides in the manual are designed for use with women-only groups, but they can easily be modified for use with mixed groups. Most training material of this sort is written as if only men were likely to use it or to be trained with it; something may be gained by training men with material which was primarily designed with women in mind!

Why train men and women together?

The first and perhaps the most compelling argument is that the world of the training course should be as similar as possible to the real world in which women have to run their businesses, and the real world is a mixed world. There are more or less equal numbers of men and women in most societies, but the world of business is usually male-dominated. Women must learn to deal with men as competitors, customers, suppliers, bureaucrats and bankers; the classroom could be a good place in which to teach them to do this.

It can also be argued that the main constraint which prevents more women from starting and succeeding in self-employment is the general belief, in many countries, that women cannot successfully run their own businesses, because they are in some way 'weaker' than men. Training courses have to be widely publicized in order to attract good applicants; the general scepticism about women in business, in society at large and among many women themselves, may be reinforced by the idea that women need 'special' training, in a sheltered environment.

We saw in the previous chapter that women in fact have many special strengths which enable them to run businesses in some ways more successfully than men. Good training is designed to help people to learn with and from one another as much as from the instructor. If men and women are trained together, they will learn from each other and eventually share the strengths and overcome the weaknesses of both sexes.

Many successful businessmen, in every society, are only too happy to admit that much of the credit for their success belongs to their wife or other female partner, and many successful businesswomen are effectively supported by a man. It is all too rare for one individual to have all the skills and all the attitudes which are necessary for success in business. An effective partnership can provide the right balance of selling and financial control skills, or of technical and people management expertise, and a highly creative and innovative risk-taker often needs the restraining hand of a more

4

cautious partner, who counts the costs as well as dreaming of the profits. Some effective business partnerships of this kind, between women and men, have originated from initial meetings on management courses, and both partners can benefit from being trained together.

Finally, training resources are scarce, and it can be argued that trainees should be selected only on the basis of their likely ability to make good use of what they learn, without reference to their race, their tribe, their origin or their gender. As we saw in the previous chapter, however, there are many reasons why women's businesses are a better 'investment', from the point of view of society as a whole, than men's. Experience shows that if business training courses are open to men and women, the proportion of women who participate is usually very small. If we want to achieve a high 'return' on our training investment, we may want to train more women for business, and single-sex courses may be the best way to do this, in spite of the foregoing arguments.

Why train women separately?

Nearly everyone with any experience of running training courses for businesspeople, the self-employed or the would-be self-employed, is familiar with all-male groups, or, perhaps more frequently, with groups of twenty or thirty people, of whom four or five, or even only one, is a woman.

We have already seen that in many, if not most, countries the majority of the smallest businesses are owned or at least operated by women. If we accept that training can be of any value to small-businesspeople, we should therefore aim to train at least as many women as men. Training courses, like licences, loans and other resources, are less accessible to women than to men; this may be quite contrary to the intentions of the organizers, but the numbers of applications, and the proportion of women participants, show that it is the case. One way to overcome this, and to ensure that training is

more equitably distributed, is to run courses which are only for women.

There are also good practical reasons why training courses for women may have to be organized on a different basis than those for men. Full-time training, occupying five or six days a week, is generally inappropriate for most serious businesspeople, unless they are unemployed and are planning to start a completely new enterprise, since they must spend at least a few hours every day managing their business. Only the owners of rather substantial businesses, with supporting management staff, can afford to leave them unattended for more than a day or two at a time.

Women have different and often even more demanding constraints on their time than men. Better-off women are able to leave the care of their homes and children to servants, and this may explain why such a high proportion of the few women who do attend business training courses are from a middle-class background. Most women, however, have to cook two or three meals a day, take care of children and their homes. Many combine all this work with full-time employment, and they may only be able to leave home for an hour or so in the evenings, when their husbands have returned from their jobs. Others may be only able to get away at weekends, or at other irregular times, or it may be necessary for the course organizers to help the prospective participants to run a temporary crèche for their children.

Whatever the particular circumstances are, it is unlikely that they will be convenient for the trainers, or the same as those which men prefer. Like any provider of a service, someone who wants to offer training for women must 'segment' the market, and offer the training at a time and place which is suitable for her 'customers', the women who are to be trained.

In some societies it would be unthinkable for men and women to sit in the same classroom; for example, nursing mothers may have to bring their babies and feed them during the course, and this may make it difficult for men and women to be together. Some men may also be unwilling or unable to share in taking care of young children; if the participants organize a crèche as part of the training, men are unlikely to do their share of the work.

Women also tend to have different training needs to men. Most women are involved in trading, handicrafts, food preparation and service and in activities related to clothing, such as weaving, knitting and sewing. There are very many exceptions, of course, but practical businesspeople are impatient of examples which do not relate directly to their own interests. Metalwork, transport services and carpentry are male-dominated activities in most countries, and very few women are likely to be interested in how to allocate the cost of welding rods or wood glue to individual jobs; the principles are of course the same as for any business, but people who have little or long-forgotten experience of classroom learning find it very difficult to apply generalized principles to their own particular circumstances.

Women also face special problems which do not generally affect men; they may not be able to take loans without the approval of their husbands, they may be reluctant to behave assertively, as is often necessary to overcome bureaucratic problems, to obtain scarce resources or to compete successfully in the market-place. They also tend to be less familiar with mathematics and technical subjects than men because many schools place more emphasis on languages and arts for girls and mathematics and science for boys.

Many women have to deal with special personal difficulties. We have already referred to the conflicting demands of the home, the family and the business, and women can gain a great deal from discussing these issues with other women, from realizing that many other women share the same problems, and learning from their fellow participants how to overcome them.

Women often have very different ambitions and expectations of their business. In theory, at any rate, men want to devote the maximum time and effort to developing their business, in order to make as much money as possible. Women are more likely to want to keep their business to a scale which will not conflict with their family responsibilities; *business* means something very different to these women than it does to most men.

Women are less likely to attend courses which are open to all, but those few who do participate are less likely to speak up, to contribute, to share their experiences and to express their problems. Some participants who remain silent throughout a course can also learn a great deal, but participative training of the sort that is most effective for learning business skills requires participation from everyone. Sadly, many women, including some who have proved themselves to be effective businesswomen, are reluctant to express their views in a male-dominated group; they can only take full advantage of participative training methods in a group of other women.

The above arguments may imply that women are 'weaker', and that they need special protection from the real world that is so often dominated by men. This may in some cases be true, but women also share certain strengths when they work together, which may be eroded in a mixed group.

Women can usually work together more effectively than men. This applies not only to co-operatives and social and community groups, but also to learning situations. Training, even for individual business, is a group activity, and women tend to be more willing to share with one another, to assist those who may be falling behind, and to subordinate their own interests to those of the group. They are less likely to want to 'show off' and have less need to prove themselves; these strengths can make a training course for women a far more effective learning experience for the participants (and for the trainers!) than a course for men or a mixed group.

Women who are in business are often more serious than men; women who have succeeded even to a modest level in a male-dominated world, and have made the sacrifices and special arrangements that may be necessary to allow them to participate in a course, are more likely to be motivated to make the best of the opportunity. They are eager to start on time, to complete assignments when requested, and not to waste time.

This manual is the result of our experience of working with a number of women-only groups, and although everyone must make their own decision, we strongly recommend at least an experiment in business training for women only.

Who should be trained, and how should they be chosen?

For whom is this material designed?

TRAINING OF THE kind suggested in this manual is not suitable for every woman who is, or wants to be, in business. Many women, for very good reasons, only expect to devote a small proportion of their time to their business, and to earn a modest supplement to their household income. It is wrong to encourage this type of businesswoman to undertake specialized training of this sort because they cannot and do not want to make full use of what they might learn, and the investment, of their time and of the cost of the training, may be out of all proportion to the returns of higher income.

The participants must also be fully literate and numerate; standards vary from one country to another, but anyone with less than about seven years' full time education, which generally means completing primary school, is unlikely to be able to take full advantage of this training. This criterion should *not* be taken to imply that illiterate women cannot make a success of their own business; in nearly every country, far more men than women can read and write, but there are nevertheless large numbers of very successful illiterate businesswomen, some of whom are millionaires. Educational qualifications are by no means necessary for business success, for men *or* women. Training of this sort, however, does require a certain level of education; this will exclude large numbers of women, but many of them may already have demonstrated that they can do very well indeed without formal business skills.

This material is intended only for training women who are already in business, on however modest a scale, or who at least have a specific idea for a business, *and* have done something towards starting it, such as acquiring the necessary skills, identifying some customers, or making and selling a few sample products, perhaps to family members or friends. Many institutions run courses for people who want, or may want, to start their own business but have no idea what business to start. This may or may not be a viable form of training, but this material is not designed for trainees of this sort.

The participants must also have some ambition, and idea about how to improve or expand their businesses. Someone who is perfectly contented with the existing volume and profitability of her business is unlikely to be sufficiently motivated to participate fully in this training; here again, this should not be taken to imply that there is anything wrong in wanting to maintain a business at its present level.

The applicants must also be serious about the course; they must want to learn, and have specific ideas about what and why they need to learn. They must have thought clearly about how they can get away from their home and their business responsibilities, and they must be protected against the very real danger of damaging or even destroying their busines by neglecting it because of the demands of the training course. Some people have an exaggerated idea of what training can do for them; we who are in the 'training business' must not oversell our product, and we must explain carefully to people who apply that the training will be a significant investment, for them as well as for the agency providing it. 'Time is money', particularly for the self-employed, and they must consider the training investment just as critically as any other.

How should applicants be attracted?

The first, and perhaps the most important, part of the selection process is to attract as many as possible of the right kind of applicants. The aim should be to publicize the course in such a way that those women whom you do not wish to attract, such as the illiterate, those without any business ideas, or those who want to come for the wrong reasons, do not even apply. This very much simplifies the selection process, since you do not have to 'weed out' those who never should have applied. You should, however, try to attract as many as possible of the kind of women you do want to attend the course, so that you can select the best possible group from them.

The training should be publicized like any product or service which is sold by a commercial firm. Many training institutions are not allowed to charge any fee, although participants should preferably be required to pay a small amount in order to ensure that they value the training. Even if there is no fee, and there may even be a stipend, participants still have to 'pay' their own time, and good applicants will realize this and have to be convinced that the training is what they need.

The publicity message should stress that the course will improve women's ability to put their plans into practice. There must not be even the *hint* of a suggestion that attendance will automatically guarantee that participants' loan applications will be approved, and the announcements must clearly state the conditions of acceptance, a well as the dates, the timing and the place, and the details of the application procedure. This can be done in a positive manner, emphasizing that the course is 'not for everyone' but only for a rather special group of women.

Posters or leaflets can be written in the form: 'Do you have a business idea? . . . Have you already taken some steps towards starting your business ? . . . Are you already in business, and do you want to improve it? . . . Are you willing and able to be at x during y period? . . . If so, apply to . . .'

The 'media', or means through which the message reaches the desired audience, will depend on circumstances. Posters and leaflets may be distributed to banks, business support agencies and women's groups. It may be possible to use the radio or the newspapers, and representatives of the training institution should try to address meetings of women's associations or other groups where there may be potential applicants, or people who are themselves in touch with businesswomen. This will put the message across more effectively than the 'mass media', and it will also provide an opportunity for the trainers to improve their contacts in the business world.

Management training institutions are themselves often very badly managed. It is vital, both in the interests of efficiency and in order to demonstrate that the trainers can do what they try to teach others to do, to ensure that the application forms are readily available, that the timing of the complete operation from the initial publicity to the start of the course is calculated to allow sufficient time for letters to reach their destinations, and to allow the women time to organize their business and home affairs for their absence. A suggested schedule is given at the end of this section.

The selection procedure

If the publicity message has been put across properly, most of the applicants will fit the basic criteria for acceptance; this makes it all the more important to select the best ones to actually attend the course.

Applicants should be asked to complete an application form, in whatever language is most familiar to them; the information requested will obviously vary, but the following deails should be included:

○ Name and mailing address, any telephone contacts etc.
○ Date and place of birth
○ Educational record, how many years of full-time schooling
○ Details of any vocational or business training courses attended (Some people go from course to course without ever applying what they learn; they should be discouraged)
○ Family situation, numbers of children or other dependents

○ Details of any jobs held at present or in the past
○ If already in business, nature of business, approximate monthly revenue, ideas for expansion or improvement
○ If planning to start a business, what business, what has been done so far, why was this selected?

The form should also state the period when the interviews will be held, and stress that applicants should not attend for interview unless they are requested in writing to do so.

These completed application forms should then be carefully assessed; the information itself, and the way it is put across, and the neatness of the presentation should all be considered. If some of the applicants are likely to be personally known to the selectors, the application forms should be numbered and the names removed before they are assesseed. If there are large numbers of apparently qualified applicants, it may be necessary to adopt a simple marking system in order to select a shortlist. The training material is designed for a group of twenty or, at the most, twenty-five women; the numbers to be interviewed should preferably not exceed twice the final number who will be able to attend.

Some trainers like to use written tests as part of the selection procedure, but experience suggests that these are a poor indicator of business potential. Women with more education are likley to do better on such tests, and are not necessarily the best businesswomen, and psychological tests of 'entrepreneurial potential' are notoriously difficult to administer and to interpret.

At least fifteen minutes should be allowed for each interview, with five minutes for the interviewers to discuss each applicant before seeing the next one. There should, if possible, be at least three interviewers, preferably women themselves, and they should agree on a common set of criteria before they start. In general, business or related experience, apparent self-confidence, clarity of ideas and a history of persistence in overcoming obstacles should count more than educational qualifications. These are of course more difficult to assess, but the interviewers should be sure to ask questions which probe each of these characteristics, while at the same time putting the applicant at her ease.

In some cases it will be clear from the outset that the applicant would not be able to cope with the training, and should not be accepted. The interviewers should not dismiss such an applicant without a hearing, and should take the opportunity to give her some useful practical advice about what to do next, where to go for other more suitable forms of training or assistance, and so on. Every applicant should feel that she has gained something from the interview.

All applicants must be informed of the final decision as quickly as possible, and it should be possible to include in the letters to those who have not been accepted a summary of the advice that they were given in the interview. It can be particularly useful to refer such people to other sources of assistance.

Those who *are* accepted should receive clear instructions on when and where to present themselves; they should also be asked to bring information about their existing or prospective businesses, copies of their accounts if they have them, samples of the products if they are easily portable, and so on. This will help to ensure that all participants learn as much about each other's businesses as possible, so that they can advise each other and even do business together after the training.

Timetable for recruitment and selection

The complete sequence as outlined above must be carefully planned, and sufficient time must be allowed at each stage to allow applicants to be informed, to communicate with the training institution, and to plan for their absence from home during the course if they are selected.

It is unlikely that a course can be properly

organized unless the initial announcements and publicity are started at least sixteen weeks before the planned starting date of the course itself; this of course means that the details of the course, such as funding premises, instructors and so on must have been finalized well before that.

This may seem to be a very long lead time, but even this assumes efficient and rapid decision-making, and speedy, reliable, mail services; this sixteen week lead time has been estimated as follows:

Publicity to be exposed in appropriate places	2 weeks
Prospective applicants apply for application forms	1 week
Application forms sent to applicants	1 week
Applicants fill in application forms	1 week
Application forms returned to training institution	1 week
Short list selected for interview	1 week
Short-listed candidates informed of interview date	1 week
Interviews take place	2 weeks
Final selection is made	1 week
Selected participants are informed	1 week
Interval to enable participants to prepare	4 weeks
Total	16 weeks

If all the prospective applicants live within each reach (easy for *them*) of the training institution, or if they all have access to a reliable telephone service, the times allowed for communication can obviously be reduced, but due account must be taken of the many demands on women's time, and of the inevitable bureaucratic delays. Many training programmes fail to recruit the people who could make the best use of them purely because the recruitment programme is badly planned.

READ THIS!!!

If you are planning to use the training guidelines given in this book, make sure that your participants are selected according to the selection criteria given on page 8! One of the main reasons why training courses are unsuccessful, of little benefit to the trainees and frustrating for the trainers is bad selection of trainees.

Remember: you will need at least *FOUR MONTHS* between the day you decide to run a course and the day it starts!

How to use this manual

THE COURSE MATERIAL in this training manual consists of session guides for twenty-nine separate sessions, together with handouts for many of them. The session guides give detailed instructions for each session in the course. Many trainers are not familiar with material of this sort, and it is important to be clear about the following points regarding adaptation of the material, preparing yourself for each session and the actual conduct of the session.

Adapting the material

You should first read through the complete set of session guides and decide what parts of it are appropriate for the particular group of women whom you are to train. It is possible, though unlikely, that the complete course can be run as outlined in the guidelines, without any modifications except for the obvious changes to names and currency.

It is more likely that:

○ only certain sessions or parts of sessions can be used
○ modifications will have to be made to the sessions which will be used
○ some entirely different sessions will have to be included, to cover topics which have been omitted from this guide, such as the rules and regulations applying to new businesses, taxes and so on.

Go carefully through the material that you plan to use, and ensure that names, currencies and other aspects are changed, particularly in the exercises, handouts and case-studies. Think of locally familiar examples to illustrate the points made during the session, and make a note of them in the margin of the session guide. Do not treat this manual as a book which should be respected and taken as the source of everything you need; it is a resource, to use or not to use as you think fit, and you should 'make it your own' by writing in it, adding to it and, eventually, discarding it because you

have developed your own personal version which is fully appropriate for the women with whom you are working.

Remember that the best examples, exercises and case-studies come from participants' own business experiences. Be ready to replace the case studies and examples given in these guidelines with examples drawn from the participants themselves.

The session guides do not represent 'finished products'; we ourselves continually change and improve them whenever we teach with them. You, too, are certain to be able to improve the structure and content of the sessions when you are preparing to teach and when you are actually working with this material in the classroom.

Preparing for the sessions

Do not fall into the trap of believing that you need less time for preparing because you have pre-prepared guidelines. The participative method which is the basis of this material requires you to be ready for any possible response to your questions; every participant has her own views, and in most sessions there are not right or wrong answers. Your task is to elicit and guide participants' contributions, and to help them to share their views in such a way that each participant evolves her own understanding of the particular topic, built on what her colleagues and you have to contribute.

Be sure to have the right number of copies of the properly modified case-studies or exercises ready for distribution at the right time. If you wish, prepare flip chart sheets, transparencies for overhead projection or other visual aids in advance but be ready to modify these in the light of participants' contributions.

Equipment

The session guides mention equipment such as the overhead projector (OHP), but the only equipment you really need is a blackboard. The handouts, suitably modified, should be typed and duplicated before the course begins, and this can be done by a local printer or typing service (preferably one owned by a woman!) if you do not have suitable facilities at your institution.

Your institution should, in fact, make the maximum use of local women-owned businesses for the provision of all kinds of services, such as catering, folders and stationery, accommodation and so on. The most direct way of assisting a business is to buy from it, and if their prices and services are competitive such suppliers can be a powerful demonstration of women's business success.

The sessions where small group preparation is suggested should be used not only to teach the topics which they cover but also as an opportunity to develop participants' self-confidence and ability to make effective presentations; this is an important part of business success. The groups can be given OHP transparencies to present their conclusions, they can use sheets of wrapping paper or blank newsprint, or they can even use portable blackboards, or sections of the classroom blackboard if it is large enough. Elaborate educational equipment such as a video recorder is useful, but by no means essential, and it can form a barrier between the participants and the instructor. A well-managed participative learning session held under a tree without even the benefit of tables and chairs can be a great deal more effective than a poorly-managed session using all sorts of equipment!

Conducting the sessions

At the beginning of each session you should have a clear idea of the conclusions to which you wish to lead participants, but you must also be ready to follow a quite different line if this appears appropriate. At the end of the session, participants should feel that they themselves have produced whatever conclusions they have reached. You, the trainer, will have done your job well if your own contribution has been tactfully to steer the participants, while they feel that they are in fact in charge.

Ensure that every participant understands what is being said; some women learn without making any pesonal contributions, while others tend to dominate the sessions, without themselves learning anything. It is your task to moderate the proceedings, so that everyone gets an opportunity to contribute, and those who do not understand, and are too shy to admit it, are identified and assisted as needed.

When dividing the group into smaller subgroups, be sure that everyone has a chance to learn and to contribute her views. When participants are working in groups, it is particularly important to ensure that any figure work is not done by one member who already has the necessary skills, while the others learn nothing.

Some trainers believe that participative sessions such as these are far easier for them than traditional lectures, because most of the ideas are elicited from the participants rather than being stated by the trainer. They are wrong; sessions such as these require more rather than less preparation if they are to be effective. The trainer must have the confidence to admit that she, too, can and must learn, with the participants, rather than pretending that she knows everything and they must only learn from her.

Duration of the sessions

Each session guide gives the estimated duration of the session, based on our experience. When you prepare a session you should split it into its different steps and activities, estimate the time for each of these steps, allow enough time for questions, discussions, group work and report-back. Take the total of your estimates as being the time for each session, rather than relying on the times given in the manual.

The actual timetable must, of course, be designed to be convenient for the women who are attending the course. At the end of this section we give some suggestions for possible schedules, but every trainer must put together a timetable herself which fits the material she proposes to use, and, more important, fits into the time that the women have available.

Handouts

Summary handouts are included after most session guides. These should be suitably changed where necessary, reproduced and distributed to participants at the *end* of the session to which they refer.

Guest lecturers

This course is designed to enable women to learn new skills and to change their behaviour so that they are more likely to make a success of their businesses. They also need to learn about the resources and the constraints in the business environment, and you should try to invite representatives from business support organizations and local or national government officials responsible for business licences, taxes, safety at work, product standards and so on. You will, in any case, be inviting bankers for the final session, when the women present their business plans, but it may also be useful to invite one or more representatives of banks or other relevant financial institutions to describe their requirements and services.

Presentations from such outside visitors can achieve a number of objectives:

○ The participants will learn about the services and regulations which affect their businesses.
○ You, as a business trainer, will be able to update your own knowledge and thus be better equipped to teach and advise businesspeople.
○ The participants will be able to establish initial contacts with the people from whom they may later want to obtain assistance.
○ The visitors themselves will be able to learn from the participants, particularly

about the special problems that affect women in business, and how their organizations can overcome them.

It is important to brief such visitors carefully; the trainer must sit in on the session and tactfully ensure that participants are given an opportunity to ask questions, and that the content of the session is appropriate and comprehensive. It is vital that you should not treat such a session as an opportunity for a break from the training course; your presence, and your interventions, are as necessary now as they are in the sessions which you yourself conduct.

Individual counselling and small group sessions

In addition to full class sessions, you may also wish to organize individual or small group sessions, to allow participants to exchange ideas and learn from one another in a more informal way than is possible when the whole group are all together, and to discuss particular problems with participants who may be unwilling to discuss them openly with a large number of people.

You may find it desirable to timetable a number of such sessions, focusing on different topics where the participants want more individual attention. For small group sessions, the participants should be divided into sub-groups of no more than four women; each should have a counsellor, who is willing and able to commit the necessary time to the task.

If there are enough instructors or other staff who are in close touch with the course you may use them as counsellors; if not, you should ask members of the group who appear to be more confident in the particular topic to act as counsellors. If you do this, be sure that as many of the participants as possible have the opportunity to serve as counsellors, in order to avoid giving the impression that some participants are 'better' than others.

It should also be possible to arrange individual meetings with participants who need special instruction on particular topics, and the small group counselling sessions will show you when this is necessary. It is important to remember that starting and running a business, particularly for a woman, involves every aspect of her life; her family, her social responsibilities and her own personal feelings about her role in society. This can involve very severe problems and conflicts, and the participants should be given the opportunity to share these in whatever forum they find most acceptable.

The enterprise experience

'The Enterprise Experience' is an action-oriented training instrument which has been included in this manual; the 'experience' runs through most of the course as it is presented in this manual, and the sessions are placed at appropriate stages. It is probably an unfamiliar type of training exercise, and therefore merits separate introduction. Unlike most forms of business training, where participants discuss, learn about or 'simulate' something, in The Enterprise Experience participants experience the tasks involved in starting and running a small business by actually *doing* it.

The Enterprise Experience involves several steps which can be summarized as follows:

The Enterprise Experience is introduced and the participants are then given an evening or a weekend to generate business ideas, to decide whether they want to run the business alone or with others and, if the latter, to make up their teams. In past training courses, participants have run laundries, taxi services, shoe-shining services, beauty salons, groceries to provide goods not available on the campus, discotheques, and many others, but it is important not to suggest ideas.

During a second session, participants present their business ideas and discuss their feasibility with the rest of the group, and this is followed by a session on how to prepare a business plan. Participants are then given some time to carry out a brief market survey and to prepare their business plans. The business plans are then presented to the 'bank', and the businesses can, if they wish, obtain loans to finance their operations.

Participants then actually run their businesses, selling to their colleagues and others, and keeping the necessary records. They then prepare their final accounts, calculate the profit or loss, repay the bank if a loan was taken, and present their final results to the rest of the group. Pripes can be given, for example for the business which made the highest profit per head.

The whole experience provides a valuable and entertaining thread through the course, and it will be clear from the above outline that it provides an opportunity for participants to practise what they have learned in other sessions in a real, even if very small-scale, situation.

You should probably only include it if the course is to be run on a full-time residential basis, since it is heavily dependent on out-of-hours working and on the group being together all the time.

If all or a large majority of your participants have substantial experience of running their own businesses, the Enterprise Experience is less likely to be useful than if the majority are new to business, and are only developing their initial business ideas during the course.

The Enterprise Experience can also be 'extracted' from this manual and used as a part of other courses; it has been used with success in the past in business awareness courses for young people, entrepreneurship development programmes, business trainer training courses and training courses for people responsible for small business promotion programmes, such as bankers, extension staff and policy makers.

Timetable suggestions

THIS MANUAL IS a resource, and you should use the sessions, or parts of sessions, in any way you think fit. It is unlikely that many readers will want to run the complete course as it is given, without any additional sessions or field visits, and without any omissions, but we have provided some suggestions, more as a basis to work from and to amend than as a model to be followed.

The minimum time required for one session in this manual is 45 minutes. We have based our suggestions for a timetable on this minimum period. Our experience tells us that in one day it is advisable to have not more than eight such 45 minute periods. This does not mean that you have to have eight different sessions during one full day, because most sessions last at least 90 minutes, that is two 45 minute periods; one session may last even a whole day. Sometimes it is advisable to have a short break, for example 5 minutes, after a 45 minute period, and a longer break after 90 minutes. But participative training involves participants in a variety of activities; they are working in small groups and so on, so they may not feel the need for regular breaks.

On the following pages you will find an example of a timetable for a four week full-time course (three weeks residential, and one week field investigations between weeks two and four). This timetable leaves enough room for additional sessions, field visits and the like. It is laid out in such a way that if you copy it and cut out the boxes, you can use it for preparing your own timetable (and if you do not close all the windows and turn off the fan you will have a great time hunting bits of paper . . .). Each box represent a 45 minute period. Each session is numbered, to remind you of the sequence in this manual. As we said before, this does not mean that you have to follow the sequence but you may have to change those session guides you want to include because many of them refer to previous or forthcoming sessions.

You can, of course, run this course during evenings or weekends. If you conduct the course during weekends you should split it into its four components (You and Your Business; What Do You and Your Customers Need; Financial Management; Planning Your Business) and fit each component into one or two weekends.

FOUR WEEK FULL-TIME COURSE

Week 1

Time	Monday	Tuesday	Wednesday	Thursday	Friday
09.00–09.45	1 Introduction	5 Meeting a Successful Business-woman	9 Resources	12 Envelope Game	14 The Marketing Mix
09.50–10.35	1 Introduction	5 Meeting a Successful Business-woman	9 Resources	12 Envelope Game	14 The Marketing Mix
11.00–11.45	1 Introduction	6 Business Ideas	10 Finding out about the Market	12 Envelope Game	15 Personal Selling
11.50–12.35	2 Enterprise Experience I	6 Business Ideas	10 Finding out about the Market	12 Envelope Game	15 Personal Selling
14.00–14.45	3 Enterprising Women	6 Business Ideas	11 Enterprise Experience IV	13 Costing and Pricing	*****
14.50–15.35	3 Enterprising Women	7 Enterprise Experience III	11 Enterprise Experience IV	13 Costing and Pricing	*****
16.00–16.45	4 Successful Business-woman	8 Enterprise Experience III	11 Enterprise Experience IV	13 Costing and Pricing	*****
16.50–17.35	4 Successful Business-woman	*****	*****	13 Costing and Pricing	*****

Week 2

Time	Monday	Tuesday	Wednesday	Thursday	Friday
09.00– 09.45	16 Basic Business Records	17 Cashflow	19 Balance Sheet	*****	23 Business Plan Introduction
09.50– 10.35	16 Basic Business Records	17 Cashflow	19 Balance Sheet	*****	23 Business Plan Introduction
11.00– 11.45	16 Basic Business Records	17 Cashflow	19 Balance Sheet	*****	24 Preparing Business Investi- gation
11.50– 12.35	16 Basic Business Records	17 Cashflow	*****	*****	24 Preparing Business Investi- gation
14.00– 14.45	16 Basic Business Records	18 Profit and Loss Account	20 Break Even Point	22 Enterprise Experience V	*****
14.50– 15.35	16 Basic Business Records	18 Profit and Loss Account	20 Break Even Point	22 Enterprise Experience V	*****
16.00– 16.45	16 Basic Business Records	18 Profit and Loss Account	21 Uses and Sources of Money	22 Enterprise Experience V	*****
16.50– 17.35	*****	*****	21 Uses and Sources of Money	22 Enterprise Experience V	*****

Week 3 = Business Investigation

Week 4

Time	Monday	Tuesday	Wednesday	Thursday	Friday
09.00–09.45	25 Report Back	27 Completing Planning Workbook	27 Completing Planning Workbook	28 Practising Presentation Skills	29 Bankers' Panel
09.50–10.35	25 Report Back	27 Completing Planning Workbook	27 Completing Planning Workbook	28 Practising Presentation Skills	29 Bankers' Panel
11.00–11.45	26 The Impact of your Business	27 Completing Planning Workbook	27 Completing Planning Workbook	28 Practising Presentation Skills	29 Bankers' Panel
11.50–12.35	26 The Impact of your Business	27 Completing Planning Workbook	27 Completing Planning Workbook	28 Practising Presentation Skills	29 Bankers' Panel
14.00–14.45	26 The Impact of your Business	27 Completing Planning Workbook	27 Completing Planning Workbook	27 Completing Planning Workbook	29 Bankers' Panel
14.50–15.35	27 Completing Planning Workbook	27 Completing Planning Workbook	27 Completing Planning Workbook	27 Completing Planning Workbook	29 Bankers' Panel
16.00–16.45	27 Completing Planning Workbook	27 Completing Planning Workbook	27 Completing Planning Workbook	27 Completing Planning Workbook	*****
16.50–17.35	27 Completing Planning Workbook	27 Completing Planning Workbook	27 Completing Planning Workbook	27 Completing Planning Workbook	*****

Evaluation

Evaluation is often treated as something that has to be done to satisfy other people, such as donors, rather than as a continuing process which everyone should engage in, whatever they are doing, in order to improve their performance.

Every trainer evaluates her work all the time, consciously or not, by observing her trainees. If they look sleepy, she tries to wake them up, if they look puzzled, she tries to clarify what she is saying and if they look bored she tries to make the session more interesting. This is a continuing and automatic feedback process, through which we all modify our behaviour. Most trainers also do their best to obtain informal feedback after each session by talking to the participants and judging what changes, if any, should be made.

Informal evaluation of this kind is probably the most valuable because it can immediately lead to improvements. You should also obtain a rather more formal view of participants' opinions by asking them to fill in a very simple evaluation paper at the end of each day, or certainly each week. This need be no more than a handwritten sheet which rates each session A, B, C or D, 'Excellent', 'Good', 'So-so' or 'Waste of Time', or you may prefer to ask for separate opinions of the content and the presentation. It is important that this should be written and anonymous, so that participants can give their own views rather than being influenced by an articulate minority, and so that it encourages frank criticism, which is, after all, the most valuable form of feedback.

At the end of the course, participants should be asked to fill in a more comprehensive form and to write down their comments on the duration, the location and the administrative arrangements, as well as stating what topics should have been given more or less time. *After* they have written down their views, you should encourage a more general discussion, based on your first reading of their written evaluations.

Participants' opinions of the course during or immediately after it are clearly only a short-term substitute for what really matters, which is the extent to which they are able to use what they learn in order to start or expand their businesses. The final results, in this sense, will not be known for many months or even years after the course has finished, but if at all feasible you should try to bring together as many as possible of the group six months or a year after the course. This will not only provide you with an opportunity to find out what they have done, and their views as to how the course helped them, but it will also provide the women with a chance to share their experiences and to renew business contacts. It is quite common for participants in courses of this type to form an association afterwards; a formal reunion meeting organized by the trainer can provide a good way of keeping such an association together.

You, the participants, and whoever has paid for the course if the women themselves have not covered the full cost, should want to know if it has been a good 'investment'; businesswomen invest in a machine only if they are confident that it will 'pay for itself' in improved earnings, and courses should be judged by the same standard.

If you are proposing to run many such courses, you should try to carry out a real 'cost-benefit' study of the first one, by estimating the income of the particpants and any employees before the course, and then repeating the exercise, say a year after the course. Ideally, you should try to isolate the effects of the course by comparing the participants' progress with that of a similar group of busineswomen and their employees over the same period. This is not easy, but it has been done with businesswomen's courses, and is the best way of finding out if the course has been a good investment.

Perhaps the most important thing to remember is that you and the participants should be aware that the training is expensive, for them in terms of their time if nothing else, and that you, the trainer, have a responsibility to give good value for money, just like any businesswoman.

Course introduction

PREPARATION
1. Prepare a name card for each participant which they should place in front of them on the table.

2. Prepare one copy of the timetable for each participant; or pin a timetable that is large enough for everybody to see on the wall.

3. Prepare the classroom: arrange tables and chairs in a U-shape or in a semi-circle.

DURATION
135 minutes, including a 'defreezing' game.

NOTE If circumstances and time allow, it may be appropriate to have a brief 'ice-breaking' or 'getting to know one another' game before the 'formal' sessions begin. This might be a game where participants have to memorize each other's names or where each participant has to ask another participant for some information about herself, in order to 'break the ice' and to make sure that participants become a group from the very beginning.

Two suggestions for 'ice-breaking' games or activities are given at the end of the chapter. You may know others that are better suited to your circumstances.

SESSION GUIDE

1. After welcoming all participants to the programme, tell them that this opening session has three purposes:

   o The first is to introduce them to the objectives of this course, and the sequence of the programme.

   o The second is to enable them to get to know one another.

   o The third is to enable them to realize that this training course will be different from most school or training situations they have experienced before: we are not here to listen to lectures given by teachers who may not know anything about the realities of business, but we are here to share our problems and our experience, and together to find solutions; the trainers are only 'facilitators' in that process.

2. Ensure that any arrangements for participants such as accommodation, travel, and funding are all satisfactory; they cannot learn effectively if they are worried about money, their families, their sleeping facilities or food. It is important that participants should feel from the beginning that these aspects of the programme are being taken care of just as much as the learning.

3. Stress again that participants are likely to learn more from one another than from the trainers; it is therefore important from the outset for everyone to be fully acquainted with one another, and to know what each has to offer.

4. Divide participants into pairs, including yourself and any other trainers who may be present. Ask one member of each pair briefly to give the following information to the other:

- What her business or proposed business is.

- Whether the business is a part-time or full-time activity (if it is a part-time activity, what other work the person does).

- How long she has been in the business.

- What changes (very briefly) she proposes to make in her business in the coming twelve months.

- Specifically, how she hopes the course will help her to achieve these changes.

5. Ask each person to introduce her partner to the class. After each introduction summarize the following information on the board, or on a large sheet of paper (you will need this information later on):

- Name

- Major type of activity/ies being undertaken

- Learning expectations

6. After each woman has been introduced by her partner, refer to the information on the board and stress the breadth and variety of activities and experience.

7. Now ask each participant to write down on a piece of paper what she is BEST at and what she is WORST at; allow two or three minutes for this. Then go round the room asking each participant in turn to say what she is best and worst at, and list these on the board.

8. Attempt to 'match' the strengths and weaknesses, showing where possible that some participants' weaknesses are matched by others' strengths; summarize the major weaknesses, and relate them to the learning expectations already listed on the board.

9. Distribute copies of the complete timetable, or refer to the timetable on the wall or board, and go through it briefly, session by session, explaining what the objectives are and how the programme links together. Relate the sessions to participants' learning expectations.

Invite questions and ensure, if necessary by asking participants direct questions about the programme, that they all understand what is involved, and who is responsible for what.

Ask participants to comment on the programme, and invite suggestions for change. Show that you, the trainer, are sincere in your desire that the participants should 'own the course', by responding positively to practical suggestions.

10. If appropriate, invite participants to elect a chairwoman, and possibly other office holders if they think fit, to act as a channel of information between the group and the training institutions. The women may also want to form committees for different purposes. Ask them to carry out the selection in any way they please. Write the results on cardboard or paper and place them somewhere where they remain visible to everybody for the duration of the course.

Suggestions for Ice-breaking Games

'SILLY SALLY' and 'BIG BETTY'

All participants sit or stand in a circle. Each should think about one adjective to describe herself which starts with the same letter of the alphabet as her name. The facilitator begins by introducing herself (for instance 'I am Big Betty'), then the woman to her right repeats 'Big Betty' and introduces herself in the same way. In the same way each woman has to repeat all previous names and introduce herself. There will be lots of confusion and laughter, but at the end the women will know most, if not all, of the names.

BLIND INFORMATION

All the women sit in a circle. One woman is introduced to the others and then blindfolded. She is then given the name of one of the participants – whom she must not be familiar with – and asked to describe the physical characteristics (how tall, shoe-size, weight and so on) of this participant. In this way, half of the participants are introduced and blindfolded one after the other, describing the other half of the participants. Clearly for the last ones it will be an easy task, but at the end each woman will not only know names, but will also be able to put faces (and even shoe-sizes) to the names of most of the other women.

The Enterprise Experience I

INTRODUCTION: GENERATING THE BUSINESS IDEA AND IDENTIFYING THE PEOPLE TO DO IT

PREPARATION

1. Prepare a copy for each participant, or write down on big sheets the content of the following handouts

– Introduction to the Enterprise Experience.

– Presentation of Business Ideas.

2. Decide on the maximum loan you are willing to give to each business that asks for a loan, and the interest rate you are going to charge. Example:
$10 per business, at 1 per cent per day or per week

3. Decide if you want to give prizes, and for what.

DURATION

45 minutes, followed by a reasonable period for thought and discussion, such as a weekend or a free evening.

NOTE: In the first section of this manual you will find introductory notes for The Enterprise Experience. You should read them before you start preparing this session.

SESSION GUIDE

1. Tell participants that the objective of this session is to introduce them to the Enterprise Experience and its sequence, and to enable them to link the Enterprise Experience to what they learn during the whole training course.

2. Ask participants what they think is the best way of learning. Some at least will come up with the answer 'by doing'. Participants may in the past have experienced training games and simulations, where they pretended to be doing things, or played games which in some way simulated aspects of reality.

   Tell them that they are about to start something with similar objectives but with a different approach: every one of them will, during the period of this course, start a business, raise finance, produce and sell goods or services, repay any money they have borrowed and retain any remaining profit.

3. If this is a training programme for people who are already in business they may doubt the usefulness of such an exercise since they are already 'doing it' in real life.

   Explain that there are nevertheless three reasons for them to go through the Enterprise Experience:

   o Not all of them may have been involved in their businesses long enough or intensively enough to realize fully the relation between what they will be taught during this course and their own business.

○ The Enterprise Experience will, step-by-step, be accompanied by sessions about the different aspects of running a business, like book-keeping, market-ing, costing, and so on; it is easier to learn these skills by performing them AT THE SAME TIME.

○ Learning should also be fun and the Enterprise Experience is fun.

4. Participants will probably express doubts and confusion: how can they start a real business in this training situation, where will they raise capital, what will happen if they fail, who will buy their products, what kind of buisness will it be? Stress the following points:

○ The participants will have to generate their own ideas for businesses. In pre-vious courses, trainess have organized taxi services, run a laundry, provided photographic processing, typing, baby-sitting, consultancy, entertainment, and so on.

○ Trainees have successfully participated in this experience all over the world. It can be done.

○ Participants may conduct their businesses individually or in groups.

○ The training institution will offer a banking service, providing loans (the max-imum amount per business and the interest rate should be mentioned here) on the basis of persuasive, well-presented proposals.

○ Participants will be expected to give the bank some collateral, such as a watch, some books, clothing or other items which could, if necessary, be sold to repay the loan in the event that they do not repay, for whatever reason.

○ Any profits earned will belong to the participants; if they cannot repay their loans, they will have to do so from their own pockets, or forfeit the security, or it will have to be sold and the proceeds used to repay the loan, with any balance only being given back to the borrower.

○ In addition to the profits, which will be theirs to keep, the training institution is offering a prize(s).

(For example, for the business which achieves the highest net profit plus wages per owner, and/or for the best kept business books. Another prize can be given to the 'most friendly' business or the one with the most unusual business idea, or the one with the best promotion strategy. The winners of such additional prize(s) should be selected by the participants themselves by secret ballot)

5. Distribute the handout 'Introduction to the Enterprise Experience', or display the prepared sheet of paper, and ask participants to copy the five steps.

Go through the five steps and relate them to the timetable of the whole training course, and to the other sessions within the course. Make sure that each particip-ant has understood that this is not a simulation exercise, but a real business, with real profits or losses for its owners.

6. When deciding whether to work alone or with others, participants should consider the following points:

- Personal friendship is not the same as business partnership.

- Decision making is easier and quicker when only one person has to make the decisions.

- Have you got all the skills you need? Who else does have them? Could you work well with her?

- How will you deal with the wages, and how will you distribute the profit or loss if you are working with others?

- If you want to invest your own money, do you have enough? If not, could you persuade your proposed partner(s) to share the risks?

- Will there be a boss or team-leader? Who will that be?

7. This evening/weekend, participants will have to decide what to do, and whether to do it alone or with others.

Distribute the handout 'Presentation of Business Ideas', or display the information and ask participants to copy it.

Each business has to fill in this sheet, or present the required information in written form for the next Enterprise Experience session. One representative of each business will be asked then to present the business idea to the rest of the group. Not more than five minutes will be available for each presentation, including discussion.

Introduction To The Enterprise Experience

The best way of learning something is to DO IT. During this training programme participants are therefore asked to start little businesses, raise finance, produce and sell goods or services, repay any money they have borrowed and retain any remaining profit.

The Enterprise Experience will be accompanied, step-by-step, by sessions on the different aspects of running a business: how to prepare a business plan, how to find out about your potential market, how to promote your business, how to prepare a cash flow forecast, how and which business records to keep, and so on.

The Enterprise Experience comprises the following steps:

1. *Introduction: Generating the Business Idea and Identifying the People to Do it*

   Generate a business idea and decide whether you will work alone or with others; if the latter, make up your team.

2. *Report Back*

   Present the idea and the team to the group, and get feed-back from your fellow participants about its feasibility.

3. *Business Plan Preparation*

   Study the market; identify suppliers; prepare a business plan and decide whether you need a loan or not.

4. *Business Plan Presentation*

   Present the proposal to the group, and to the bank, if you want a loan.

   Then plan and produce the goods or services, and sell them, keeping records as you go.

5. *Presentation of Final Results*

   Prepare accounts, calculate profit or loss, repay the bank; present the results to the group and, maybe, win a prize; describe your experience to the group.

Presentation of Business Ideas

Return a completed copy of this sheet to. . . . .

on .at .hours.

_____

Name of the proposed business: . . . .

. . . .

Name(s) of the Owner(s):. . . . .

. . . .

. . . .

. . . .

. . . .

. . . .

What good(s) or service(s) will the business offer:. . . . .

. . . .

. . . .

. . . .

. . . .

. . . .

Enterprising women

PREPARATION

1. *Invite two or three successful businesswomen, and discuss this session with them well in advance. Tell them that they are not expected to give a polished presentation of any kind but to talk freely about their experiences, so that the women participating in this course can learn from them.*

   You may feel hesitant about asking busy and perhaps well-known businesswomen to your course; in fact, these women nearly always welcome such invitations, even from trainers with whom they have no acquaintances in common. Successful businesspeople enjoy talking about their business, and helping others to succeed, even if they are potential competitors.

2. *For step 3 of the session guide (problem analysis) you need to prepare the following materials:*

   ○ *about 50 sheets of normal size paper cut to half size (you may use scrap paper with a blank reverse in order to save paper.)*

   ○ *if available: one felt pen for each participant, including guests.*

   ○ *tape, pins or whatever is appropriate, to stick some fifty pieces of paper to a wall or blackboard.*

DURATION   *90 minutes*

NOTE: If appropriate, ask your guests whether they would be willing to receive the participants for a 'field visit' to their businesses at a later stage of this course. It is often said that women in particular lack the exposure they need in order to change attitudes and to stimulate new ideas. Field visits are a way of giving them that exposure. Make sure that the visit is well organized, and give the women an assignment, such as something specific they should observe, or make them write a short 'case study' about the visited business.

SESSION GUIDE

1. After introducing the guests, explain the objective of this session:

   ○ To enable participants to identify problems women may encounter when opening and/or running a business.

   ○ To enable them to discuss ways of overcoming these problems with experienced businesswomen.

2. Distribute the paper (at least three pieces for each participant) and felt pens. Write the following statement on the top of the blackboard:

**Many women run very small business activities
but only a few expand their business successfully**

Now ask participants (and invite the guests to participate):

○ to think of at least two reasons or causes for the above statement.

○ to write each reason separately on one piece of the previously distributed paper; they should only write a short sentence or a key word, and the writing should be big enough to be read by people at the back of the room.

○ to stick the papers on the wall or blackboard.

NOTE: We have found this method of analysing a problem by asking the participants to write their suggestions on cards or pieces of paper and displaying these to be very successful on many occasions, especially during the first days of a programme, when participants are not yet familiar with one another. It ensures that everyone contributes her views and displays them to the others (and to herself), and it increases the sense of 'belonging' to the group.

---

3. After each participant has displayed her paper, the wall or blackboard will be filled with reasons or 'problems' many of which may be similar or even the same. Group the papers into the different subjects or headings. For example, causes like 'lack of money', 'cannot get bank loans', 'no capital to start business' should be grouped together.

4. Make sure that each paper is considered and that the participants agree to the 'grouping'.

At this point it may be appropriate to point out that many of the causes or problems mentioned are not only true for women but also for many small-businessmen. It is important for the women to realize that the difficulties of running a business successfully do not only derive from their being women, wives, and mothers.

5. Have participants considered that some women may not want to expand their business activities? If not, discuss this issue. It is important for participants to realize that success is related to the goal they set themselves.

6. Now invite the guests to talk about their experience, how they started their businesses and how they dealt, or deal, with problems such as those listed on the board. Each guest should not speak longer than 15 minutes. Encourage the participants to ask questions after each presentation; invite those who have buisness experience to describe how they overcame obstacles or problems like the ones mentioned.

7. Write the suggestions made by the guests and by experienced participants on the

31

board, preferably below each group of corresponding 'problems'. Your board or wall should now look like this:

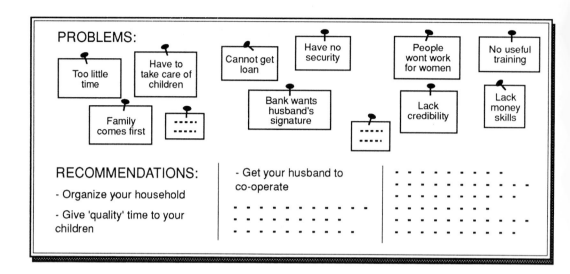

8. Summarize the session and thank the guests. Invite them to stay for some time after the session if they wish, to give the participants a chance to talk to them more informally.

> **NOTE:** NETWORKING is one important factor for business success. This course could be the beginning of a network of businesswomen in the town or region where the course is taking place. You as a trainer can encourage and promote such a network in many ways: by inviting businesswomen, as for this session; by initiating a party, organized by the participants, for all businesswomen of the town or region, and so on.

Successful businesswomen

PREPARATION   *Copy on a large sheet of paper the list of characteristics as stated on the attached handout.*

(Do not prepare copies of the handout in its present form for all participants; do that only after this session, when you have included participants' findings.)

DURATION   *90 minutes*

SESSION GUIDE

1. Tell participants that the objective of this sesion is to enable them to identify the personal qualities that are at least as important for running a business successfully as management or technical skills.

2. Ask participants to suggest why they have come on this course; what have they come to learn?

   Elicit suggestions such as: 'acquire record keeping skills', 'learn how to market my products', 'learn how to apply for a loan', and so on.

   Ask participants whether business success can be guaranteed so long as a businesswoman has all these types of skills. Are there some other abilities that are required?

3. Ask participants whether education, which is largely concerned with acquiring skills, is essential for success in running a business; are people with Ph.D. degrees or masters degrees usually the ones who make the most money by running their own businesses? Participants should appreciate that higher education is not a guarantee of business success.

4. Ask for examples of very successful people, even millionaires, who are illiterate; there are such people and they can obviously not keep records or write loan applications. What have they got, that many very well-trained or educated people have apparently not got, that enables them to be so successful?

5. Clearly there are other qualities that are at least as important, and possibly more important, than management or technical skills. The objective of this session is to identify these qualities.

6. Ask participants individually to think of one particular successful business owner whom they know personally (remind them of the guests of the last session), and then to write down *one* adjective that best describes the sort of person she or he is. Allow up to five minutes for this, and then ask for suggestions and list them on the board; do not write down different words that mean more or less the same thing, but put ticks beside the word that is already written to show how many participants suggested it.

7. Divide the group into pairs; ask them to do the following:

○ find out each other's ages

○ then the younger one should describe briefly (for not more than three minutes) one occasion in her career when she achieved something important to her. What did she actually *do* on that occasion?

○ the older one should listen carefully, and then write down *one* adjective or phrase that best describes the way the younger one *behaved*

○ then the older one should similarly describe something she did in her career

○ and the younger one should similarly listen and write down one adjective or phrase she thinks best decribes her behaviour.

If necessary, give participants an example, like the following:

Younger women tells older woman, 'I wanted badly to participate on this course but I almost failed because I could not find anyone to take care of my two little children. It took me six weeks and I went to see all kinds of people, day-care centres and so on. Finally my cousin Betty agreed to stay with the children.' Older woman listens and then writes down: 'she did not give up' or 'she is persistent' or 'she persuaded her cousin'. (But: 'she was lucky' is clearly not a behaviour!)

Allow not more than six minutes for this task, and then ask participants to read out what they have written. Add the words or phrases to the list already on the board, again avoiding duplications but showing how many times each word or general concept is suggested.

8. Discuss the resulting list: Remind participants of the objective of this session (to identify qualities that are important for successful business) and eliminate words that do not appear to relate to successful business or career behaviour as such. Stress that successful businesspeople are not necessarily pleasant people, or honest people; avoid the impression that a successful businesswoman is a perfect woman.

9. Write up or display the previously prepared list of common types of behaviour of successful businesspeople, as attached to this session guide. Tell participants that the types of behaviour listed there have been identified by psychologists and others who have studied successful businesspeople, mainly successful businessmen. Encourage discussion as to whether this list is or is not basically similar to the one the group members have themselves developed by describing each other's behaviour and that of successful businesspeople they know.

If the list developed in the session includes characteristics which are significantly different from those in the attached list, and all participants are agreed that they are important, amend the attached list. Likewise, if there are some of the characteristics which participants themselves have not come up with earlier in the session, discuss whether they are relevant or not; if the group feels strongly that these characteristics are not relevant, in their situation, exclude them since participants must feel that the list is *theirs*.

10. If time allows, encourage participants to recall situations in their own lives when they achieved something important because they displayed one or more of these characteristics.

11. Ask participants to use this course as an opportunity to find out whether or not they themselves have the listed characteristics, maybe to enhance them, or to find out about their strengths and weaknesses. They should also help one another to improve their behaviour for business success.

Successful Businesswomen

There are certain personal qualities that are at least as important as, and possibly more important than, management or technical skills. When talking to and observing women who run successful businesses, one will find that they display most, if not all, of the following types of behaviour:

- they are persistent
- they grasp opportunities
- they make problems into opportunities
- they take moderate and informed risks
- they try to do things more efficiently
- they strive to improve quality
- they are persuasive
- they network
- they try their best to keep promises
- they set goals for themselves
- they plan ahead, and monitor the results
- they rebound from failure
- they invest in tomorrow rather than spending today
- they are unconcerned about what others think of them
- they are enthusiastic
- they are self-confident

Some people say these qualities can be developed, or at least improved, by training, while others say that people are born with them, or that they are acquired during early childhod; it is certainly true, however, that you can gain by finding out whether or not you have these characteristics, so that you can try to develop those you have not, or at least recognize your own strengths and weaknesses.

Meeting a successful businesswoman

PREPARATION

1. Invite a successful businesswoman to your session well in advance. She need not be dramatically successful although she should be at least as substantial a businessperson as the most successful of the participants. What is most important is that she should be articulate and willing to talk honestly and openly about her experiences, without idealizing herself and saying what she thinks people think about her, as opposed to describing what she actually did.

Discuss the session with the guest well in advance, and tell her that she will not be expected to give a polished presentation of any kind. All you want is for her to talk freely about certain incidents in her business career, so that the participants can learn from what she has done.

2. Prepare one copy of the handout Successful Businesswomen (previous session) for each participant.

DURATION

90 minutes

SESSION GUIDE

1. Tell participants that the objective of this session is to enable them to meet and objectively appraise a woman who has succeeded in business.

   This session is not intended to show participants what they ought to be, but to give them an opportunity to meet and objectively evaluate a woman who has succeeded in business, and in particular to compare this woman with the list of qualities identified in the previous session.

2. Before the session each participant should have received a copy of the handout 'Successful Businesswomen' prepared at the end of the previous session. Explain that you will ask the guest to describe certain experiences she has had, and participants will be expected to make notes whenever they consider that the guest's description of her behaviour shows that she displayed one of the listed characteristics. They should also note when the guest has displayed characteritics which are not on the list but which participants feel should be included.

3. After introducing the guest (who may, of course, be already known to some of the participants), ask her to tell the group about an occasion when she solved a particularly difficult problem; ensure that she focuses on what she *did*, rather than on what she thought about or thought that other people thought of her.

   It may not be necessary to interrupt at all, other than to bring the story to a close; it may, on the other hand, be necessary to steer the story on to the right track, and to help the guest to recall what actually happened.

4. Depending on how long this story takes to tell, you may then ask her to describe other occasions, such as:

   ○ when she felt she failed to do something she wanted to do

   ○ when she felt particularly pleased with what she had done

   ○ a particularly important milestone in her busines

   ○ when she took a risky decision

   ○ when she had to get help from others.

   The nature of the occasion is less important than the fact that the guest can talk about it clearly and openly; ensure throughout that the participants are remembering to make notes, as well as paying attention to the speaker.

5. A more structured approach is to ask the guest to describe her business career from the beginning, going into particular detail when the situation was particularly difficult, and stopping at major decision points. At these points, ask participants to say what they would have done, and then ask the guest to comment on their suggestions, and to compare them with what she actually did.

6. About thirty minutes before the end of the session, draw the guest's stories to an end, and invite participants to ask questions, relating to what she has been saying, or to their own business problems and opportunities.

7. After the guest has left, or at the beginning of the next session (even the next day), 'process' the session by asking participants to say which characteristics the guest displayed, and what particular event seemed to illustrate the characteristics.

   If one or more of the characteristics appears not to have been displayed, discuss possible reasons why this may be so. Does this represent a weakness, has she displayed it in other ways, or is its absence balanced by other particularly strong characteristics that may not be on the list but that seem to be related to her success in business?

   Ask participants to compare their own behaviour in similar situations; would they have behaved differently or in the same way? Would the result have been more or less successful?

Business ideas

PREPARATION

The preparation depends on what the trainer chooses to do during this session.

DURATION

135 minutes or more

> **NOTE:** If you have followed the selection criteria given in the first section of this manual, all your participants will have a business idea and will have even taken steps towards starting a business. But their ideas may have been generated in a narrow environment; the women may have had little exposure to sources of ideas.
>
> This session is about being creative, about adapting ideas, and generating new ideas. It is also a challenge to you, the trainer, and to your own creative thinking.
>
> The session guide is therefore not structured in the usual way; we only give you a few ideas of what you could do to achieve the following objective:
>
> > To enable participants to reconsider the business
> > opportunities that lie in their own skills and in
> > their immediate environment.
>
> If the Enterprise Experience is included in this course, and some participants have not yet identified their businesses, they may use this session to find an idea (which will have to be presented in the next session.)

SUGGESTION 1

BRAINSTORMING

If all or most of your participants have not started any business activities, you could have half an hour or so of 'brainstorming', followed by an evaluation of the ideas. For example:

○ Give participants a key word (e.g. 'egg'; 'rain'; 'flower') and ask them to name any product or service they can think of that relates to this key word (e.g. chicken, egg-cups, selling eggs, fried eggs; rain-coat, umbrella, rubber-boots, and so on). There are no limits to their imagination, all suggestions are accepted, even the most crazy ones. Insead of a key word, you can also select a product area (e.g. 'food-processing'), which will involve more ideas and need more time.

This technique is used by many companies to produce new product ideas. It is based on the belief that creative ideas can be generated if the atmosphere encourages creative thinking and evaluation and judgement are suspended. The rules are:

○ no evaluation of any kind is permitted

○ participants should be encouraged to think of the wildest ideas possible

- encourage a large number of ideas

- encourage participants to build upon or modify the ideas of others.

Write every suggestion on the blackboard. Allow at least twenty minutes for this exercise (the more the better); ask for a large number of ideas.

When enough suggestions have been made, each suggestion is analysed as to whether it appears to be a feasible one: would people like to buy it? Would the raw material to make it be available? Do any of the women have any skill to make or provide it?

The products or services selected as 'possibly feasible' can then be examined in more detail. This can be done for example through a SWOT-analysis.

SWOT-ANALYSIS

S trength – W eaknesses – O pportunities – T hreats

Consider the following aspects related to a product, a service, a new business:

- The strength of the woman (or group) who plans to or is producing the product or providing the service, in relation to that product or service; for example: she has the skills to produce it, she knows the market very well, she has easy access to suppliers.

- The weaknesses of the woman (or group); for example, she does not have skills, she cannot dedicate very much time to it, she does not have premises.

- The opportunities the woman/group has with the product or service; for example, it is in demand but there are no nearby suppliers, the raw materials are readily available, banks are interested in giving loans for such an undertaking.

- The threats, for example, unforeseeable changes in politics, market demand, technologies, new competitors.

SUGGESTION 2

PROBLEMS ARE OPPORTUNITIES

Ask each participant to write down one small problem which she is facing now; it need not be a business problem and may relate to the classroom or course environment.

List them in summary on the board.

Now ask participants to suggest how each problem is in fact a business opportunity. For example:

- 'I am worried about my children at home' — a crèche

- ○ 'I am hungry or thirsty'   — a fast food or drinking stall

- ○ 'There is nowhere to wash clothes'   — a laundry service

- ○ 'It is too hot'   — fan or airconditioner installation

Stress that successful businesswomen are optimistic; they see opportunities where other people see problems.

SUGGESTION 3

MUTUAL AID

If your participants have already started a business, ask each to prepare a short (maybe ten minute) presentation of her business: What does she do? How did she get the idea? Why does she think it is a good idea? Why will people buy it? Ask them to bring samples (or photos, drawings) of their products. After each presentation there should be a discussion, and all participants should be encouraged to ask critical (but constructive, not destructive!) questions. If you have enough time you can also do a short SWOT analysis after each presentation. Plan and time the session carefully; you may have to split the group into two or three smaller groups in order to give each business enough time for discussion.

If you have individual or small group counselling sessions during this course you should ask all counsellors to participate in this session. It enables them to become more familiar with each participant's business.

The Enterprise Experience II

REPORT BACK

PREPARATION   *None*

DURATION   *45 minutes*

SESSION GUIDE

1. The objective of this session is to enable participants to present their business ideas and obtain feed-back from the rest of the group.

2. Ask a representative of each proposed enterprise briefly to tell the group the enterprise name, owner(s) and products or services to be offered. Ask each enterprise to hand in the paper with these details. Ensure that:

   o there is no impractical double use of resources (but competition is to be encouraged so two discos, two soft drink stands or two hairdressing businesses are fine)

   o any partnerships are real, in the sense that all members have agreed and there are no obvious 'passengers'

   o all participants understand that it is for real; in spite of earlier reminders, some may still believe that it is a paper exercise.

3. 'Process' the 'idea generation', either during the individual presentations or after all businesses have presented their ideas, by asking or initiating questions such as the following:

   o How did participants generate their ideas?

   o Did they 'network' by asking others for ideas, or did they rely on their own ideas?

   o How could they have improved their use of other people?

   o Are their ideas innovative or obvious?

   o Are they proposing to do ordinary things, but in a better way, by making them cheaper, more convenient in time or place?

4. 'Process' the individual/team decision, and the team selection when that route was chosen, in the same way by asking questions such as:

   o Were they able to appraise their own strength and weaknesses, in order to find out if they needed a partner?

   o To those who are going to have individual businesses: Why is it that they prefer to work alone?

   o Have they ever thought about a business partnership, in the Enterprise Experience, or in their own real businesses if they are in business already?

○ To those who have decided to form partnerships: Who were the initiators, how did the followers feel about their invitation?

○ (If relevant:) Why did they decide on a partnership in the Enterprise Experience but not in their real businesses?

○ Do any participants want to change their ideas, and/or partners, after hearing about their colleagues' ideas?

If yes: Why? Most businesses are competing for limited purchasing power and time, even if they do not offer the same products/services.

If not: Do participants feel confident that their ideas will succeed, in spite of the competition they have now heard about? If so, why? If not, why not? What can they do to improve their chances?

NOTE: This session should be followed very soon by the next Enterprise Experience session Business Plan Preparation so that participants can start working on their business plans.

The Enterprise Experience III

BUSINESS PLAN PREPARATION

PREPARATION   *Prepare copies of 'Planning Your Enterprise Experience' for each participant.*

DURATION   *45 minutes*

BUSINESS PLAN OR FEASIBILITY STUDY?

Many training programmes use the term 'Feasibility Study'. We believe that 'Business Plan' states far clearer what the objective of such a 'study' is.

This is the very first step leading participants to realize the importance and value of a business plan. When they see the document they have to complete they may feel they cannot do it. They will make mistakes, but by these mistakes they will learn. They will also be able to ask more detailed questions when it comes to preparing business plans for their real businesses.

SESSION GUIDE

1. Tell participants that this session has two objectives

   o to enable them to identify the usefulness of, and the need for, a business plan

   o and to enable them to prepare a very simple business plan.

2. Refer back to the handout 'Introduction to the Enterprise Experience' where the different steps of the Enterprise Experience are listed. Warn participants that during the next Enterprise Experience session they will have to present their business plans. For those who want to apply for a loan, the Bank will be open and a 'banker' will attend the session. The Bank is willing to provide loans up to $10 per business, at an interest rate of one per cent per day (or whatever terms you select) if the applicants present a convincing business plan and reasonable security.

3. Ask participants to name reasons for preparing a business plan, besides the above-mentioned reason of applying for a loan. Elicit suggestions such as the following:

   o A business plan can serve as a guideline for your business operations.

   o It forces you to think through, and plan properly, what you intend to do.

   o It will give you more confidence in your ability to run your business successfully.

44

- You might want someone else to put money into your business or you might want to obtain credit from suppliers; you should therefore be able to answer questions about your business.

- It forces you to investigate your potential market, and your possible suppliers.

- It provides you with more information to decide how best to operate your business.

- Once you have a plan, you have set yourself a long-term and several short-term goals.

4. After having identified these and other reasons, ask participants to suggest what information should be included in a simple business plan, in order to have a document which is useful for themselves, and also to persuade the Bank to lend money.

   Elicit suggestions such as the following, and write them on the board:

   - A statement of what product or service the business is to provide.

   - A statement of who the customers are, and why they will buy this product/service.

   - A statement of the objectives of the business.

   - A summary of the materials and equipment needed, and their sources and prices.

   - A brief description of the person(s) involved, and why she/they are likely to succeed in this business.

   - A calculation of the expected financial results of the business.

   - A calculation of the finance needed, a statement of where it is proposed to raise it, and evidence that it can be repaid on schedule.

5. Distribute 'Planning Your Enterprise Experience'. Compare the questions in the workbook with participants' suggestions on the board. They should be very similar.

   Many participants will not know how to produce a Balance Sheet; point out that the questions use ordinary language, and that they should use common sense: how much money will they need for their enterprise, how will they use it (assets) and where will it come from (liabilities)?

   Stress that learning comes through discovery; later sessions on financial management will be more valuable if participants have already grappled with the problem.

6. Tell participants that they have to prepare this simple business plan for their proposed Enterprise Experience businesses for the day before the next Enterprise Experience session. During that session (Business Plan Presentation), a representative from each business will have ten minutes to present the plan, and another ten minutes to discuss the plan with their fellow participants, and with

the 'banker'. Those businesses which want to apply for a loan can make individual appointments with the 'banker' at the end of that session.

> **NOTE:** Allow participants enough time to prepare the business plan. Use their proposed business ideas as examples during the next sessions. Use their Enterprise Experience businesses for all kinds of learning purposes during your programme!

Planning Your Enterprise Experience

NAME OF THE BUSINESS: . . . .

. . . .

DATE: . . . .

1. NAME OF THE BUSINESS: . . . .

. . . .

2. WHAT IS THE BUSINESS GOING TO DO? . . . .

. . . .

. . . .

. . . .

3. NAME/S OF THE BUSINESS OWNER/S: . . . .

. . . .

. . . .

. . . .

. . . .

. . . .

. . . .

4. IF MORE THAN ONE OWNER: WHAT WILL EACH PERSON DO? . . . .

. . . .

. . . .

. . . .

. . . .

. . . .

. . . .

5. WHY ARE THEY/YOU PARTICULARLY QUALIFIED TO RUN THIS BUSINESS?

. . . .

. . . .

. . . .

. . . .

. . . .

. . . .

6. WHO WILL BE YOUR CUSTOMERS? . . . .

. . . .

. . . .

7. WHY WILL THEY BUY YOUR PRODUCTS/SERVICES? . . . .
. . . .
. . . .

8. WHO ARE YOUR COMPETITORS? . . . .
. . . .
. . . .

9. HOW WILL YOU PROMOTE, DISTRIBUTE AND SELL YOUR
PRODUCTS/SERVICES?
. . . .
. . . .
. . . .
. . . .

10. WHAT MATERIALS AND/OR EQUIPMENT WILL YOU NEED, AND
WHAT WILL THEY COST?
. . . .
. . . .
. . . .
. . . .
. . . .

11. WHERE WILL YOU OBTAIN THE ABOVE? . . . .
. . . .
. . . .
. . . .

12. WHERE WILL YOU LOCATE YOUR BUSINESS, AND WHY? . . . .
. . . .
. . . .

13. WHAT RECORDS WILL YOU KEEP, AND WHO WILL KEEP THEM?
. . . .
. . . .
. . . .
. . . .

14. WHAT PRICES WILL YOU CHARGE? . . . .
. . . .
. . . .
. . . .

15. WHAT QUANTITIES WILL YOU SELL? . . . .
. . . .
. . . .
. . . .

16. WHAT WILL BE YOUR COSTS? . . . .
. . . .
. . . .
. . . .
. . . .

17. WHAT IS YOUR FORECAST OF TOTAL SALES, COSTS AND PROFITS
FOR THE PERIOD GIVEN?

SALES:

COSTS:

PROFIT:

18. HOW MUCH OF THEIR OWN MONEY WILL THE OWNER(S) INVEST
IN THE BUSINESS, IN CASH AND IN KIND? . . . .
. . . .
. . . .
. . . .

19. WHAT DO YOU ESTIMATE WILL BE YOUR DAILY CASH FLOWS IN
AND OUT OF THE BUSINESS?

(please attach cash flow forecast)

20. WHAT WILL BE YOUR BALANCE SHEET AT START OF THE
    BUSINESS AND AT MIDNIGHT THE DAY BEFORE THE FINAL
    PRESENTATION?

Starting Balance Sheet

How the money is used Assets	Where the money comes from Liabilities
Cash	Loan
Stocks	Owner's Investment
Equipment	Others
Others	
Total	Total

Final Balance Sheet

How the money is used Assets	Where the money comes from Liabilities
Cash	Loan
Stocks	Owner's Investment
Equipment	Others
Others	
Total	Total

21. WILL YOU NEED A LOAN? . . . .

22. IF YOU NEED A LOAN:

    FOR HOW MUCH? . . . .

    WHEN WILL IT BE REPAID? . . . .

    WHAT SECURITY CAN YOU OFFER? . . . .

Resources

PREPARATION

1. *Prepare copies of the two case studies attached to this session guide, suitably modified.*

   If no photocopier is available, write the main information and the assignments for each case on the blackboard before the start of the session.

2. *If available, have one or two big sheets of paper ready for each of the four or five work groups to present their completed assignments.*

DURATION

90 minutes

SESSION GUIDE

1. Tell participants that the objective of this session is to enable them to identify the different steps involved in starting up and operating a business, and the information that is needed.

2. Present the two case studies very briefly. Divide participants into small groups of not more than five members, so that at least two groups get the same case study. The women with some business experience should be evenly distributed among the groups.

   Distribute a copy of the respective case study to each group member, or ask the groups to copy the main information and the assignments written on the board.

NOTE: Instead of the cases presented here you may ask participants to complete this exercise for their Enterprise Experience businesses. If you do this, you may have to shorten the time for the individual presentations.

You might prefer to write up short case studies of small businesses you know, using the same assignments, and arrange visits to businesses after this session to enable particpants to find the answers to unanswered questions.

---

3. Allow about 30 minutes for the assignment. Ask one group to present their findings, and the second (and third) group with the same case study to add their findings. Encourage discussion after each case study is completed.

   Presentation and discussion of each case study should not take longer than half an hour.

4. There will be many questions:

- bureaucracy: licences and other formal requirements (what is required, where to get it)

- the shop/workshop: furniture, equipment (what is needed, where best to get it, what would it cost); facilities (water, electricity, night guard, cleaner)

- supplies: where best to get them; will wholesalers supply to the shop; where to store them

- customers: who will they be; how to attract them to the new business

- employees (supermarket): are employees required, how many, for which type of work, where to recruit them, salaries, bureaucratic requirements.

Each type of business has different requirements, and at this stage it is not important that participants produce a complete checklist of the things that are necessary to know before starting a business but it is more important that they realize that there are many questions to be asked.

5. Ask participants whether they would recommend Mary to start her business now. Certainly the answer will be: *no*. Ask them what could happen if she were to start now.

If participants recognize the need to answer these questions before Mary can start operating, then the objective of this session has been achieved. They themselves will have to answer similar questions before they can start their proposed businesses.

CASE STUDIES

In this session two case studies are introduced: *The 'New Style' Tailor's Shop of Miss Mary Green*, and *The 'Best Food' Grocery of Mrs Sara Blue*.

Sometimes it may be useful to produce your own case studies for specific teaching or training purposes, or to ask course participants to produce case studies about a business or certain aspects of a business. Sometimes it may be easier to use existing cases. There is a vast amount of literature about case study teaching and writing. There are also many books of case studies for teaching purposes. We have included a few titles in the bibliography at the end of this manual.

You should change the names given in the case studies to local, more familiar names, and make any other changes that may be necessary.

CASE STUDY

The 'New Style' Tailor's Shop of Miss Mary Green

Mary Green wants to open a tailor's shop. Sewing has been her hobby for many years, she taught herself how to make patterns, her hand-stitching is almost as perfect as machine stitching and for the last year she has been using her sister-in-law's sewing machine to sew curtains, cushion covers, pillow-cases and other simple items for family and friends, and also one or two dresses for herself.

After graduating from secondary school, Mary could not decide what to do next. Her uncle asked her to work in his shop, selling furniture, and she did so for a few months but she did not like it much, and the salary was not very good either. Some of her friends had paid her for the clothes she had made for them. She knew that there was no other tailor in her neighbourhood, and there were many people who could be her customers. She estimated that if she could make one dress a day she could earn more money than by selling furniture in her uncle's shop. She was quite sure that her sister-in-law would let her use the sewing machine until she could afford to buy her own machine.

So she decided to open a tailoring shop. The name was easy to find: 'New Style'. Now she could start her business. A friend suggested that she should have some leaflets printed, with the name of her business, her address and a price list, and distribute them at her uncle's shop and other places.

She had not thought about prices before. What should she charge? What items should she put on the price list? What did she need to know before deciding about prices? She was quite confused.

ASSIGNMENT:

○ What does Mary Green need to know before she can produce a price list?

○ What should she know before even deciding whether to open a tailoring business or not?

CASE STUDY

The 'Best Food' Grocery of Mrs Sara Blue

Mrs Sara Blue is a teacher by profession. Her husband was a quite successful lawyer but his career was brought to an end after a serious car accident a few years ago. Until then they had been able to save a substantial amount of money, which was now slowly eaten up by school fees and other expenses because Mrs Blue's salary was very low. Mrs Blue was very worried and they discussed the matter with other family members. What could they do? Mrs Blue was willing to stop working as a teacher, she was a bit tired of it anyhow after almost twenty years of service.

Somehow the idea of going into business came up. But what kind of business? Mrs Blue talked to many friends and came to the conclusion that a grocery shop, maybe even a supermarket, selling high quality food, fresh vegetables and some household goods, would be a good idea. She also found out that in one of the residential areas a new shopping centre was being built and that no other grocery was located in that area. A suitable place for a grocery shop was available for what looked to be a reasonable rent. Mrs Blue talked to wholesalers; also, one of her friends had a large vegetable farm and was interested in supplying fresh vegetables twice a week. So far, so good. But what to do next? So many things came to Mrs Blue's mind that she thought she was going crazy. She would have to sit down and make a list of all the things to find out and to do before her dream of a fancy supermarket could take shape.

ASSIGNMENT:

Help Sara Blue to make a checklist of all the things she has to find out before renting the space in the new shopping centre.

Finding out about the market

PREPARATION   *1. Prepare a list of trade promotion organizations, market research institutions, import and export organizations, local authorities, chambers of commerce/trade and the like, which can provide market information for the types of businesses your participants are interested in.*

                                      2. Prepare copies of the list for all participants.

DURATION   *90 minutes*

SESSION GUIDE

1. The objective of this session is to enable participants to find out what their customers want.

2. Remind participants that any business must be led by the 'market', that is the customers. If not enough people or none at all are interested in, or can afford to buy, the service or product a business is offering, then there is no 'market' for that service or product, and the business will fail.

   Therefore, successful business people say: The customer is King (or Queen)!

   Everything else, such as raw materials, equipment, staffing, premises, capital and so on must depend on what customers want.

3. Point out that there are two possible approaches to starting or running a business, which may be illustrated by the following imaginary statements that might be made by someone starting a dress-making business:

   > 'I can make this type of dress and I can get a sewing machine, so I shall start a business making these dresses'.
   >
   > OR
   >
   > 'People need dresses of this price and quality; I have the necessary skills and access to the equipment, so I will satisfy their needs in this way'.

   Ask which is preferable; clearly the second, which is *market* as opposed to *production*-oriented.

4. Most participants will have at least a business idea, if they have not already started a business. Use these business ideas or businesses to discuss the market versus production issue:

   (If you have introduced the Enterprise Experience in this training course, you can also use participants' business ideas for this discussion)

   Ask participants to recall why they decided to take up this or that business idea, or start the businesses they did. Discuss which of these approaches are 'market-oriented' and which are 'production-oriented'

5. Ask participants what they actually did; did anyone carry out even an informal

56

survey, or was it enough to assume that if they themselves had a problem, their neighbours, or their colleagues on the course would probably have the same one.

Stress that this may be quite adequate for the Enterprise Experience but there is a need for more information when you want to start or to expand a business, with your money and your livelihood at risk. Market studies are not just something done by large firms, or something needed by bankers as part of a business plan or feasibility study; they are an essential tool for anyone proposing to start or expand a business.

6. Ask participants how they can find out what customers want; elicit the suggestion, 'by asking them', and then elicit the two major problems in this approach:

   ○ You cannot usually ask all of them, because there are too many.

   ○ When people are asked '*Would* you buy this or that?', they may not respond exactly as they would when they actually have to decide whether to buy or not; it is easier to say 'yes' than actually to pay.

7. Deal with the first problem (You cannot ask all, because there are too many): Ask how many of the participants are left-handed; show that the proportion is probably not too different from that of the population as a whole, even though you have only asked about twenty people.

   Ask how many of the class are female; clearly this answer is not true for the population as a whole; similarly, ask how many have five or more children, or live in the capital city; elicit the comment that these answers may not be typical of the population as a whole. Ask why this is so, and elicit the suggestion that this group is not *typical* or *representative*, of the population as a whole, because they have probably been specially selected; they may come, for example, from a particularly higher-than-average income group which tends to have smaller-than-average families, or the very fact that they are in business for themselves may mean that they also have smaller families.

   Elicit the conclusion that a small *sample*, maybe no more than forty or fifty people, can give you quite accurate information about the market, so long as they are *typical* of the group to whom you want to sell your product.

8. Remind participants of the other problem: (asking people something is not the same as selling them something.) Ask for suggestions as to how this can be overcome:

   Elicit suggestions such as the following:

   ○ Try the business on a small scale, even at a loss, since information is worth money if it avoids subsequent larger losses. A restaurant's proposed food can be tried in a kiosk or market, a shop's products can be tried in a temporary stall, samples of clothes can be sold to friends or through shops on a trial basis.

   ○ Study competitors' operations; count their customers, check their prices, observe what, and how, their customers buy.

   ○ Study published data on imports and exports, numbers of vehicles, income levels and so on as indicators of the market for your goods or services.

9. Remind participants that if they have no competitors it may be because they have no market! If there are large numbers of similar businesses, this usually represents an opportunity to find out what extra service is needed, and to provide a similar product which is different and better in a particular way; what is needed has to be found out through the type of enquiry which has been suggested.

10. Remind participants who wish to undertake surveys or use questionnaires that they can get assistance from various sources; stress finally that information should only be obtained which is useful; before you ask any question, you should ask: 'What am I going to do with this information?' If you cannot say, do not waste time and money getting the answer!

Finding Out About The Market

Successful business people see opportunities, where other people see problems:

When people have a *need*, they have a *problem*.
You can *satisfy* their need, that is your *opportunity*.

But, you must be as sure as you can that you know what they need, where they are, and how they are trying to satisfy the need right now.

A market study is not a complicated expensive thing that only big companies can do, or that you only need to satisfy the bankers.

It is a practical, economical way of reducing your risk and finding out how you can help people to satisfy their needs.

But there are two major problems:

1. You can't ask *all* your potential customers, it would take too long.

2. What people *say* they will buy is not the same as what they *will* buy.

So: ask a *sample*, which is typical of the whole group, and need not be more than about fifty people.

And: whenever possible, *try out* your product or service, on a small scale, to see if people actually *will* buy it.

Sources of information

Published data: for trends, exports and imports (this does not include smuggled goods, which may be important!)

Questionnaire surveys: but try out the questionnaire first, do not try to get too much information, and be sure *why* you want to know what you are trying to find out.

Observation: assess the amount of traffic, watch the shoppers, look at the advertisements.

The competitors: how well are they doing, where are they, what do their customers think, what are their prices?

Remember: ○ if there are no competitors, maybe there is no market

○ if there are very many competitors, the market must be very big, maybe you can find a 'niche' where nobody else is selling

○ the business that everyone says you should go into today is probably the one where everyone will be losing their money tomorrow.

The Enterprise Experience IV

BUSINESS PLAN PRESENTATION

PREPARATION

1. A suitable staff member should play the role of the 'banker'; she/he should be well briefed as to the nature of the Enterprise Experience, and its objectives, and should have had the opportunity to study the proposals in advance. She/he should also be given a copy of the 'Guidelines for the Banker', attached to this session guide.

2. Collect all business plans the previous afternoon, or at least some hours before the session, allowing yourself and the 'banker' to prepare for the session.

3. Prepare some copies of the 'Loan Form', attached to this session guide.

DURATION

135 minutes (depending on the number of businesses to present a business plan)

SESSION GUIDE

1. Tell participants that the objective of this session is to enable them to explain the objectives of their business and their business plans to bankers, and other relevant people.

2. A representative of each business should make a presentation, to last at most ten minutes, supported by flip chart, overhead projecter or other visual aids if appropriate. Those businesses who are going to ask for a loan should be the first to present in order to allow time for changes if their applications are refused.

   Participants whose businesses do not need a loan, either because they need no initial capital or because they wish to finance them themselves, should still make a presentation, but to invite comments and suggestions, not acceptance or refusal of a loan.

3. Participants whose applications are refused, if any, must quickly revise their plans; this may involve revision of the presentation, change of business idea, joining another business, break up of the partnership or other changes.

   If possible, allow them to make and confirm their new plans during the session, so that everyone knows what they are going to do at the end of the session.

4. There is no reason to demand that participants should stick to their plans; some of the most successful businesses are those which change rapidly and unexpectedly in response to changes in circumstances. A businesswoman should not continue with a bad business just because she presented it to a banker and received a loan to implement it.

PRESENTATION SKILLS

Use this session to practise participants' presentation skills! It is often said one of the problems of women in business is their lack of confidence. If participants propose to run enterprises with two or more owners, encourage them to choose the less confident ones to make the presentation.

After each presentation discuss issues such as:

- the structure of the presentation
- if visual aids were used: how was the layout, were they legible?
- was the content clear?
- is the plan convincing?
- was the presenter confident, did she know what she was talking about?

5. 'Process' the experiences of obtaining information, preparing the proposal and presenting it to the banker:

- Did some participants find it difficult and even annoying to have to put figures to their ideas? Were they easily able to 'translate' comments such as 'we shall sell lots of that' into a precise figure of how many sales would be made?
- Other participants will have found it easier to quantify their ideas: are any of the partnerships made up of a 'quantative' and a 'qualitative' person?

Discuss the importance of both vision and broad concepts, and the willingness to put figures to one's dreams, to satisfy outsiders such as bankers but also to be able to manage a business successfully.

6. Ask participants how they obtained the information necessary for their proposals:

- Did they ask from one source, and then give up if they failed?
- Did they cross-check their data by asking for information from different sources, in different ways?
- What ingenious methods did they use to obtain apparently unavailable information?
- Did they obtain information which was unnecessary, and which they did not use, for the sake of obtaining it, or were they able to use all the information they obtained?

7. After this session participants will have a certain number (this depends on your timetable) of days or weeks in which to run their businesses. Ensure that everyone understands that they are expected to keep daily records, and that on the day xyz (give the date) they are expected to make a final presentation of their business results and experiences.

Guidelines For The Banker

○ Ensure that participants keep to the time limit.

○ Be as intimidating and discouraging as bank managers can be.

○ Respond positively to genuinely effective responses, and do not act defensively to possibly over-assertive behaviour.

○ Give positive and useful advice, not merely destructive criticism, and try to approve most, if not all, of the loan requests.

○ Ensure that the offered security is genuine and saleable, and seal it in a bag or other container, clearly labelled.

○ Ensure that the applicants understand their obligation, the interest added, and the strict requirement to repay.

○ Be ready to suggest alternative sources of finance, such as increased owners' contribution or external investments from friends or colleagues, if the loan is unacceptable, more than can be granted or insufficient for the needs of the enterprise.

○ Ensure that borrowers understand how interest is calculated; this should be on a daily basis, so that borrowers can reduce the cost if they repay early.

○ Ensure that borrowers retain one copy of the completed loan agreement.

Loan Agreement

Between. . . . .
and the Loan Shark Bank.

We, the undersigned, have agreed the following terms:

       Loan amount:. . . . .

       Interest rate:. . . . .
       Loan repayment schedule: . . . .

              . . . .

              . . . .

              . . . .

              . . . .

       Security:. . . . .

              . . . .

          Date:. . . . .

_____   _____

Manager, Loan Shark Bank   Representative, borrowing enterprise

- cut here -

This is to certify the receipt of the following security

. . . .

taken from the . . . .

on the (date). . . . .

The security will be returned as soon as the loan has been repaid.

_____

Manager, Loan Shark Bank

The envelope game

PREPARATION

1. *For four groups of five participants each you need the following material and facilities:*
   - *1500 sheets of A4 paper (approximately 21cm × 28.5cm) which should, if possible, be neatly-cut pages from old magazines or surplus scrap; it may be printed on both sides but should not be creased.*

     If A4 paper is not available, you must experiment with whatever is the local available paper size, and change the dimensions accordingly, putting them in inches if necessary. The sheets must all be of the same size, since the final dimensions of the envelopes determine their acceptability.
   - *20 pens*
   - *12 pairs of scissors*
   - *12 rulers with centimetre markings*
   - *12 glue sticks or other suitable adhesives*
   - *1 sample envelope*
   - *1 copy of the Instruction Notes for each group*
   - *3 copies of the Order Form for each group*
   - *3 copies of the Finance Sheet for each group*
   - *1 copy of the Observation Guidelines for each observer*
   - *separate space for each group to allow independent work*
   - *at least one table for each group*
   - *board or flipchart to present the results*
2. *Ask four of your colleagues or four participants (or more, if you have more groups) to act as observers during the game, and give each a copy of the Observation Guidelines and Briefing Instructions attached to the session guide.*
3. *Prepare a sample envelope according to the instructions given on page 67.*

DURATION

135 minutes, or more if you have more than four groups (and, therefore, need more time for discussing the experience)

SESSION GUIDE

1. Tell participants that the objective of this session is to enable them to experience the importance of proper planning, efficient use of resources and high quality standards for the success or failure of the business.

2. Distribute the Instruction Notes, read them aloud, and make sure that each participant understands them. Show the sample envelope; ensure that it is of excellent quality.

3. Divide participants into groups of not more than five. Assign each group a workplace in the training room, or in several smaller rooms, if possible.

4. Assign one observer to each group.

5. Distribute one Order Form and one Finance Shdet to each group.

6. Now ask participants to start the first planning round. Each group should experiment, formulate their plans, and discuss how best they can achieve their goals. They have 30 minutes for planning. At the end of this period each group must have completed its order form and submitted it to the trainer.

7. Ask the observers to join the groups. Make sure that they have read the Observation Guidelines and know, what to observe.

8. While the groups are planning their work, prepare a desk for the receipt of order forms and the handing out of materials.

    Have some 20 sheets of paper (5 for each group) ready for the groups to experiment. Do not distribute them; give them only to groups that ask for paper to experiment. The paper should be marked in such a way that any envelopes made during this planning can easily be distinguished from the envelopes made later.

    In the same way, allow each group to use one item of all available materials (i.e. one pair of scissors, one ruler etc) during this planning round, but only if they ask for it.

9. After the 30 minutes planning period make sure that every group has submitted an Order Form, including the production commitment, and has received the requested materials.

    The order forms stay with the trainer.

10. Now ask the groups to start the first production round. Ask the observers to rejoin their groups. Time this round carefully to last exactly 30 minutes.

    Participants are not allowed to use their own pencils, rulers and so on.

11. While the groups are producing envelopes, prepare a 'quality check desk', and a sheet of paper for each group indicating

    ○ number of envelopes planned

    ○ number of envelopes delivered

    ○ number of envelopes accepted

12. After exactly 30 minutes of production time ask the groups to stop working and the observers to collect the envelopes produced.

65

13. While participants take a break, check the quality and quantity of each batch of envelopes and write the figures on the previously prepared forms.

    Envelopes that do not fulfil the requested standards should definitely be rejected!

14. Reconvene the groups, tell them the results of the quality check and ask them to complete their calculation of profit or loss according to the Finance Sheets handed out with the game instructions. Allow 10 minutes for this task.

15. Now start the processing of the game. First ask the observer of one group to report what she/he observed; then ask the respective group to summarize their experience; discuss questions such as

    ○ Did you achieve your goal? What were your difficulties?

    ○ Did everything go as planned? What went wrong?

    ○ Did you try to reduce quality standards: with what results?

    ○ What have you learned that will help you to do better in the second round?

    Process the results of each group in that way.

    Allow 10 minutes for the presentation and discussion of each group.

16. Now start the second round of planning and production:

    This round is exactly like the first round. Each group is again given 30 minutes to plan their production; financial forecasts are similarly prepared.

    The actual production should again be carefully timed for 30 minutes.

    You can turn this 'game' into a more realistic business situation if real money is introduced: participants have to buy tools and raw materials with their own money and you/the training institution pays for each accepted envelope.

17. After the second production round when all calculations of profits or losses have been made and results have been presented and discussed, summarize the experience gained during the game and discuss with participants whether the objective of this session has been achieved or not.

NOTE: If you do not have enough time for the full game, you can shorten each round to, say, 15 or 20 minutes, with the exception of the first planning round, which should be 30 minutes.

If you shorten the time, you will have to change the prices of material and equipment. For the 30 minutes round they are calculated on the basis that a group can make at least three envelopes per minute (i.e. 90 envelopes in 30 minutes), and that if they buy 100 sheets of paper and the maximum amount of all equipment, and if they produce 90 envelopes up to the requested standard, they can make a profit of $0.90.

Do not forget to change the hand-outs accordingly!

HOW TO MAKE A SAMPLE ENVELOPE

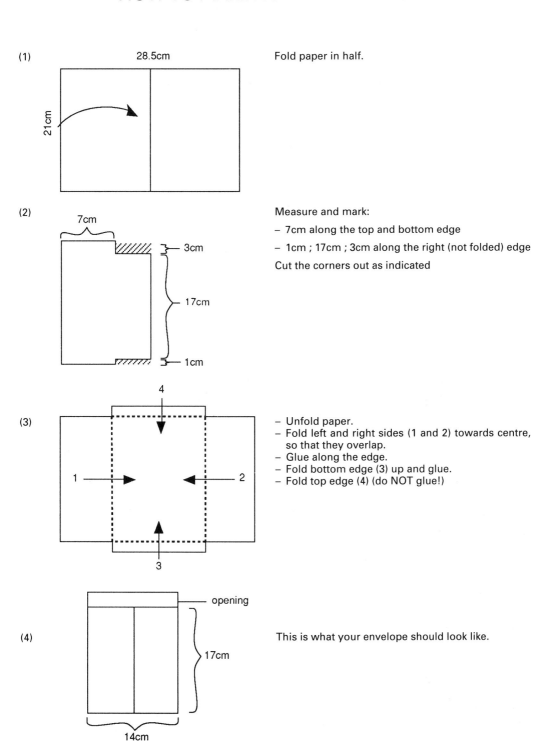

(1)
28.5cm
21cm

Fold paper in half.

(2)
7cm
3cm
17cm
1cm

Measure and mark:
– 7cm along the top and bottom edge
– 1cm ; 17cm ; 3cm along the right (not folded) edge
Cut the corners out as indicated

(3)
4
1
2
3

– Unfold paper.
– Fold left and right sides (1 and 2) towards centre, so that they overlap.
– Glue along the edge.
– Fold bottom edge (3) up and glue.
– Fold top edge (4) (do NOT glue!)

(4)
opening
17cm
14cm

This is what your envelope should look like.

The Envelope Game

INSTRUCTION NOTES

Planning and running a business is not simple, even if you produce a simple product, such as, in this case, envelopes.

If you want to be successful it is very important to plan properly, and to work efficiently with the least waste of resources.

The exercise is done in two rounds:

1. Planning: 30 minutes

2. Production: 30 minutes

1. PLANNING

The most important part of the planning is to find out how much you can produce during the 30 minute production round. Based on this, you will know which and how much equipment and material you will need.

The market is clear: Your customer is this training institute.

Since they rely on you, you must give a binding commitment as to how many envelopes you will deliver.

The contract conditions are as follows:

$0.11 per accepted envelope

$0.03 per extra envelope (exceeding the agreed number)

$0.04 penalty per envelope that you fail to deliver.

The specifications are:

○ size 17 x 14cm (+ or – 2mm)

○ tidy and well-glued

○ not glued on the inside

○ exact cutting

○ exact folding

○ clean appearance

The training institute is quality minded and only accepts envelopes fulfilling those specifications.

THE ENVELOPE GAME – INSTRUCTION NOTES (continued)

The equipment and raw materials available, and their prices are specified on the Order Form.

At the end of the 30 minute planning period you have to submit your Order Form including your binding commitment.

If you have enough time, use the upper part of the Finance Sheet to calculate whether your production will be profitable.

2. PRODUCTION

For the production of envelopes again you have 30 minutes. At the end of this period all envelopes have to be submitted to the Quality Control Desk.

The Quality Controller will tell you how many envelopes have been accepted and how many rejected.

Once you have this information, use the lower part of the Finance Sheet to calculate your financial results.

The Envelope Game

ORDER FORM

Item	Maximum quantity available	Quantity ordered	Price per item	Total costs
Paper	no limit	. . . .	$0.01	. . . .
Scissors	3	. . . .	$0.60	. . . .
Rulers	3	. . . .	$0.20	. . . .
Pens	5	. . . .	$0.20	. . . .
Glue	3	. . . .	$0.70	. . . .
Labour (per group member; per 30 minutes)		. . . .	$0.50	. . . .
			TOTAL	. . . .

We can promise to deliver . . . . envelopes according to specification within 30 minutes.

We agree to pay the penalty as given in the contract.

Signed . . . . (Representative of Group . . . . .)

The Envelope Game

FINANCE SHEET

Forecast:

Expected Sales	$ . . . .
Less Costs (initial investment)	$ . . . .
	_____
Profit	$ . . . .

Results:

Sales:

Planned envelopes at $0.11	$ . . . .
Extra envelopes at $0.03	$ . . . .

Costs:

Planned Total Costs $ . . . .

Additional Unforeseen Costs

. . . .	$ . . . .
. . . .	$ . . . .
. . . .	$ . . . .
. . . .	$ . . . .
	_____

Total Unforeseen Cost $ . . . .
                                                         _____

Total costs
(Planned plus Unforeseen) $ . . . .
                                                         _____

Sales less Costs = Actual Profit or Loss $ . . . .

The Envelope Game

OBSERVATION GUIDELINES

1. Read the Instruction Notes carefully.

2. Join your group, observe what they do, listen to what they discuss, take notes.

3. Some points to watch during the planning round:
   - What does the group do at the beginning of this round?
   - Do they choose a leader, does someone take the leadership without being asked?
   - How is the actual planning done?
   - Do they ask to see the sample again?
   - Do they ask for paper and equipment to experiment?
   - Do they plan to divide the tasks?
   - Do they talk about/plan quality control?

4. Some points to watch during the production round:
   - Do they organize themselves and the material and equipment in order to have an efficient production flow?
   - Do they work according to plan?
   - What is actually happening during the production, who is doing what?
   - Does someone watch the time, control the quality?

Costing and pricing

PREPARATION   *1. The day before the session: distribute the case study 'Catherine's Dresses', so that participants can complete the assignment in advance.*

DURATION   *180 minutes*

NOTE: If you are not familiar with this topic, re-read the handouts 'How to calculate costs' and 'How to choose the right price' before planning the detail of this session.

SESSION GUIDE

1. The objective of this session is to enable participants to calculate the costs of their products or services and to identify and apply different ways of pricing.

2. If some participants have not read the case study 'Catherine's Dresses', ask one participant to read it aloud.

   Ask a volunteer to suggest what is the cost of each dress which Catherine makes, and elicit, by reference to other participants if necessary, the following summary of the costs:

   (Do not introduce any other concepts such as fixed or variable costs or depreciation at this stage)

MATERIALS:
- cloth
- lining
- thread
- buttons
- zips

Cost of 50 dresses = $425
Cost of 1 dress   = $425 divided by 50   = $8.50

LABOUR:

- Catherine makes 1 dress from 2 to 6 p.m., that is
  2 dresses in 1 working day
- she works 25 days per month, that makes 50 dresses
  per month (2 dresses times 25 days)
- she needs a 'salary' of $100 per month for her living expenses;
  $100 labour per month divided by 50
  dresses per month, equals labour costs per dress of $2.00

SUPPLIES:

- needles
- machine oil
- chalk

Cost for 6 months = $42, equals costs of $7 per month
($42 divided by 6 months)
Supplies of $7 per month divided by 50 dresses made
per month equals costs of supplies per dress of $0.14

TOTAL COST PER DRESS $10.64

3. Ensure that all participants fully understand the way in which this cost has been calculated.

Ask other participants to comment on the figures which Catherine has produced as a basis for costing her dresses; elicit criticisms and questions such as the following:

○ By allowing for 25 working days per month, and 8 working hours per day, she has allowed no time for selling, for buying material, or other ancillary tasks which are essential if she is to run a business.

○ There is no allowance for wastage of material, for maintenance of the machine beyond the supplies she has allowed for, or for transport expenses in buying material or delivering the dresses.

4. Ask participants what would happen if Catherine had to rent the sewing machine for $25 per month.

Elicit the suggestion that the cost per dress made would increase by $0.50 ($25 per month divided by 50 dresses made per month).

We know that Catherine did not rent the machine but bought it for $600. Is that not a cost? What happens if the machine breaks down after the ten years it is supposed to last? Introduce the concept of depreciation as a way of ensuring that enough money is available for replacing equipment.

○ The machine cost $600.

○ It will last 10 years; at the end of 10 years the machine will be worth almost nothing:

○ Every year its value decreases $60 ($600 divided by 10 years).

○ Every month it decreases by $5 ($60 divided by 12 months).

Ensure that all participants understand this, by asking what would happen if every month for ten years Catherine puts $5 in a savings account. Elicit the suggestion that she would have saved $600 (plus interest) at the end of 10 years, which would enable her to buy a new machine when the old one is worn out.

Stress the doubtful value of depreciation as a way of ensuring that enough money is available for replacing equipment, particularly in times of inflation and when technology is changing. It is nevertheless necessary to make some allowance for the cost of using equipment.

The $5 per month or $60 per year is a cost, in the same way as renting a machine would have been a cost.

5. Ask participants to remember how the cost of making one dress was put together. Elicit that the cost of a product is composed of three elements:

o Raw materials: (in Catherine's case the material, buttons, zips)

o Direct labour: this is the cost of all labour that is directly involved in the production of the product (in Catherine's case her own wage)

o Overheads: these are all the other costs which cannot easily be allocated to each item that is produced, like rent, electricity, water, transport, sales costs (e.g. posters for sales promotion), administration costs, indirect labour (e.g. the salary of the manager, of a secretary, accountant, store-keeper and the like), and the costs of interest on loans and depreciation, (in Catherine's case the supplies and the depreciation)

6. Ask participants to suggest what is basically different about the cost of materials from the other costs; elicit the suggestion that the cost of materials varies directly with the numbers of dresses which are made, whereas Catherine will have to earn $100 per month however many dresses she makes, the machine will depreciate at the same rate and the supplies are likely to cost more or less the same.

Show how costs can therefore be roughly divided into 'fixed costs', which remain the same whatever the level of production is, and 'variable costs', which vary directly with the amount of goods produced.

The variable costs of a business are raw materials and wages for workers who are paid on 'piece work' basis, that is according to how much they produce. Some overheads may be variable (e.g. the costs of maintenance of a machine may depend on how frequently the machine is used).

The fixed costs of a business are most of the overheads and also the direct labour, if wages are paid on a regular basis (like Catherine's own wage).

If participants have started their own businesses or if you have used the Enterprise Experience, ask them to suggest what are the fixed and variable costs for these businesses. Discuss issues such as their own labour and wages paid to others, and show that except for casual labour which is recruited for specific tasks and paid day by day, most labour costs, including, in particular, that of the owners themselves, can be regarded as fixed.

7. Ask participants to repeat the calculation of costs for Catherine's dresses, but this time with more realistic figures. Let everyone decide what 'realistic' means: 2 or 8 hours for selling the dresses every month, 10 or 15 per cent wastage, and so on. The cost of depreciation will have to be included. The cost of transport has to be guessed. Ask them also to divide the costs into fixed and variable costs.

Allow participants about 20 minutes for this task.

Compare and discuss the different results. Encourage discussion about the costing of the products or services they produce in their own businesses or in their Enterprise Experience businesses.

8. Ask participants what price Catherine should charge. Elicit the suggestion that she should add some percentage or profit margin, say 5 to 15 per cent to the final costs of the dresses. This is called 'cost plus' pricing, and is a very common

pricing method when there is no direct competition with which to compare prices.

Ask participants in what other way Catherine could estimate a reasonable price for her dresses. Elicit the suggestions that she could compare her dresses with those of other tailors, find out what others charge and then, taking into account the costs and the quality of her dresses, fix the price below, above or at the same level as the competitive dresses.

9. Ask participants what Catherine should do if she finds that comparable dresses are apparently being offered to Mrs Grace's boutique at $10.50. Elicit the suggestion that she should closely examine the variable costs (for example, the quality of the material and the amount of material used per dress). Her fixed costs (that is, her own salary and the supplies) are already very low, and remember that her costs of $10.64 that Catherine calculated (see step 2 of this session guide) do not include transport, maintenance or depreciation.

10. Ask participants to suggest ways in which Catherine might be able to reduce her costs, and thus to meet the competitive price. Their suggestions should include:

    ○ using less raw material by cutting more economically

    ○ redesigning the dresses to use less material or to save cutting or stitching time

    ○ buying material from less expensive suppliers, or in larger quantities to get quantity discounts (BUT, it is vital to avoid tying up money in stocks of material which may never be used)

    ○ by producing (and selling) more than 50 dresses per month, for the same wage, and thus spreading the fixed costs over more dresses, so that the fixed cost per dress will be lower.

    Ask participants to estimate the cost reduction Catherine would achieve by producing 55 or 60 dresses per month, instead of 50. Elicit the answers as follows, and ensure that all participants understand the principle:

    Fixed Costs = $107: @ 50 dresses, fixed cost per dress = $2.14

    @ 55 dresses, fixed cost per dress = approx. $1.95, reduction = 19 cents

    @ 60 dresses, fixed cost per dress = approx. $1.78, reduction = 36 cents

11. Stress that the best way to meet lower priced competition is often not to cut costs, which often leads to lower quality, but to increase quality, even if this slightly increases costs, so that customers are willing to pay more for your products: refer back to the sessions on marketing, and ask particpants for suggestions as to how a tailor such as Catherine might improve her dresses and obtain higher prices. Elicit ideas such as:

    ○ improve the designs

    ○ offer a wider range of colours and sizes

    ○ label the dresses, and build a quality 'image'

    ○ provide protective and attractive packaging.

12. Ask what she should do if it appears that competitors are pricing similar dresses at $11 or more. Some participants may suggest that she should still charge as little as possible in order to get the order.

    Elicit through discussion that a low price is not necessarily more competitive because it may be associated with low quality. Catherine should charge 'what the market will bear', and should use her costs only as a 'floor' beneath which she should not allow her prices to fall since she will otherwise be losing money and would be better occupied working for even a very low wage, or doing nothing at all.

13. If time allows, it may be useful to ask participants to calculate Catherine's costs again, with different figures and additional costs such as rent and electricity, or including an employee and increased production.

How to Calculate Costs And Prices

Every businesswoman needs to know what the costs of her products or services are. By knowing your costs you have a basis on which to decide your sales price and your pricing policy. Only by knowing your costs are you able to calculate whether each product is making a profit or a loss.

The cost of a product is composed of different elements:

- ○ Raw materials

- ○ Labour, or better: Direct Labour
  This is the cost of all labour that is directly involved in the production of the product.

- ○ Overheads
  These are all the other costs which cannot easily be allocated to each item that is produced like rent, electricity, water, transport, sales costs (e.g. posters for sales promotion), administration costs, indirect labour (e.g. the salary of the manager, secretary, accountant, store keeper and the like), and the costs of interest on any loans and depreciation of equipment.

The costs of a business can be divided into the following categories:

- ○ Variable costs
  These are all the costs that vary with the amount of goods produced (raw materials, e.g. cloth for a tailor, feed for a poultry business, food for a restaurant, petrol for a taxi; wages paid according to work done.)

- ○ Fixed costs
  These are all the costs that remain the same whether a business produces one item or one hundred. (Most of the overheads, and also the direct labour, if it is paid on a daily or a weekly basis and the numbers employed do not change directly according to the amount produced.)

Some cost items are 'semi-variable', in that they may not double or halve if production doubles or halves, but they do change. Every businesswoman must examine how the costs of her business vary according to production, and use the information to calculate her costs and thus to set prices.

CASE STUDY

Catherine's Dresses

Catherine was good at dress design and cutting, and she started her business with one sewing machine, which she bought with $600 which she had received when she took early retirement from her job. She had bought the best machine she could find, and her friends told her that such a machine would last at least ten years of hard use. She also had a small pension, and reckoned that she could survive if she could earn £100 a month from her tailoring business.

She made a sample of her latest design, and took it to Mrs Grace's boutique, where many such products were sold. Mrs Grace was very impressed with the design and quality, and said that she hoped she would be able to sell lots of such dresses to her customers. She asked Catherine what price she wanted to charge. Catherine realized that she had not decided on a price, so she made an excuse and said she would come back tomorrow with a quotation.

When she got home she wondered what she should do; she knew that she had spent $425 on cloth and other materials such as lining, buttons, zips and thread, and that this was enough for fifty dresses, but beyond this she had no idea. She had also spent $42 on needles, machine-oil and chalk, which she thought would last for six months, and since she worked from home she had no other expenses.

Catherine thought she could think better about the problem of pricing while she was working, so she decided to make another dress. She was used to working eight hours a day, for 25 days a month, and it was 2p.m. when she started. By 6p.m. she had cut and sewn and completely finished the dress, but she still had no idea what price she should ask Mrs Grace to pay.

ASSIGNMENT

o What is the cost of each dress that Catherine makes?

o What price should she charge for each dress?

o Does she need more information and if so what?

The marketing mix

PREPARATION   *Prepare one copy of the handout 'Marketing – Points to Remember' for each participant.*

DURATION   *90 minutes*

SESSION GUIDE

1. At the end of this session participants should be able to identify the basic marketing mix, the four 'Ps' (Product, Price, Promotion, Place), and they should also be able to identify the Unique Selling Point of their actual or proposed businesses.

2. Ask participants to suggest what it is that people are *really* buying when they buy the products of their or other businesses; their answer will probably relate to the item as such. A tailor will say 'clothing', a restaurant owner will say 'food' or a pickle-maker will say 'pickles'.

   Refer to this training programme: what is it that they, the trainees are 'buying' with their time and the fees they paid? Is it just 'training', or are there some other *benefits*, which they expect to get and which are the real reason for their coming to the course?

   Elicit the suggestion that they have come to the course to *learn*; go further behind this and elicit the more basic *benefit* which is to be (more) successful businesswomen.

3. Go back to the example of products or services offered by participants in their own businesses, or the Enterprise Experience businesses. Ask participants to look around at one another: what was each of them *really* buying when she bought whatever she is wearing today?

   Elicit the suggestion that people buy clothes for the .sake of protection and decency. Then ask participants to look again at the clothes they are wearing: if they had only bought them for the sake of protection and decency, would there be so many different designs or colours? Would not a flour bag with a hole in the end and two holes in the sides do just as well? Why do people not buy identical clothes if all they want is to be decent and protected against the weather?

   Show that people buy clothes for very many reasons, in addition to protection and decency, and sometimes inconsistent with these benefits.

   Elicit suggestions such as:

   ○ to acquire status
   ○ to show membership of a certain group
   ○ to acquire confidence
   ○ to become attractive

4. Refer to other businesses such as a restaurant, or a hairdresser; elicit motives for purchasing their goods or services, such as:

○ to meet people
○ to relax
○ to overcome boredom
○ to forget troubles

5. Now describe a business, such as a restaurant or a tailor's shop, whose owner has recently invested heavily in production improvements, but without any corresponding increase in sales.

Write the outline details on the board, and ask participants to suggest ways in which the owner might put matters right. Elicit as many suggestions as possible, and list them in four different columns, without, at this stage, explaining the basis of the categorization.

6. The final lists might read as below, but WITHOUT the headings at this stage:

PRODUCT

Higher quality
Bigger quantities
Better finish
Better packaging
Better labels
More varieties
Different colours

PLACE

Longer opening hours
Better decoration
Different location
Home delivery
Faster service

PROMOTION

Advertising
Signboards
Competitions
Editorial mentions
Different names

PRICE

Higher prices
Lower prices
Longer credit
Quantity discounts
Special offers

7. Ask participants to suggest why you have divided the suggestions into the four different lists; guide them to the understanding of the four different 'Ps', and write in the headings as above.

Introduce the concept of the marketing mix, using the analogy of a dish where the final outcome can be varied to suit the taste of whoever will eat it, by adding more or less of the various possible ingredients.

Illustrate this by drawing a pie diagram, and show how one

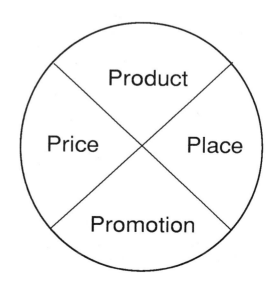

segment can be increased or decreased but that this will affect the size of the segment taken by each of the others.

8. Confirm participants' understanding by asking them to suggest which of the four 'Ps' is most emphasized in each of the following cases (or find more suitable cases for your own environment):

   o Nescafé (The Promotion, because the Price is high, but the makers have developed a 'brand image' through advertising, so that people insist on it.)

   o A newspaper vendor (The Place, because people will only buy a newspaper where it is convenient; they will not walk more than a few yards to get one.)

   o A special dress (The Product, people will pay a great deal, and travel a long way, to get the dress they want.)

   o Rationed goods (The Price, because it is usually inconvenient to get them, and the quality may be low, but the price means that it is worth while, nevetheless.)

9. Ask participants to suggest alternative methods for each of the four 'Ps,' that may not have been mentioned in the context of the business which you used as an example at the begining; use the same headings, and ensure that items such as trade fairs, in-store displays, sales agents, radio, television and newspaper advertising, public relations campaigns and so on are included.

10. Ask participants to think about their own actual or proposed products or services; what is their marketing mix, and how should they improve it in order to sell more, to attract more customers?

    If you have used the Enterprise Experience in this course, you can also relate this question to these businesses.

11. Introduce the notion of the Unique Selling Point or USP which each business must have if it is to survive and prosper.

    Ask participants to recall the last time they bought anything, whether it was a newspaper, a snack or something more important such as a dress or a bag of flour; why did they buy that product, from that supplier?

    Elicit reasons such as:

    o The place where the product was sold was convenient.
    o It was available at the right time for them.
    o The price was the lowest available.
    o The product was available at all, being in short supply.
    o The person who sold it was friendly and pleasant to deal with.
    o The place where it was sold was a pleasant one.

    Show that for each person, at that time and place, that supplier was unique in the sense that she decided to buy there.

12. Ask participants what is the USP of *their* business which will lead their customers to buy from them. Allow them up to ten minutes to write down why they think their customers (will) really buy from them.

Ask them to read out their conclusions about their own products; discuss them, compare the different USP suggestions for the same 'products'; show how restaurant meals, or cooking oil, can actually be serving quite different needs, depending on their location, price level, selling environment, 'image' and other aspects of the marketing mix.

Marketing – Points to Remember

THE FOUR 'Ps': PRODUCT, PLACE, PROMOTION AND PRICE

THE PRODUCT (or service) – its presentation, its packaging, its varieties, its design, its colours, its styles, its materials.

THE PLACE – where it is bought, the physical and the social barriers, home delivery, the distribution channels, transport, the atmosphere, the decoration.

THE PROMOTION – advertising, free publicity, personal selling, shows, exhibitions, in-shop displays, mailings, phone calls.

THE PRICE – the amount, the status and quality meaning of high prices, the discounts, the credit terms.

All these, and many more, are the *ingredients* of the 'mix' that you must select in order to provide your chosen customer group with the best 'bundle' of values; there is far more to it than just price and quality!

THE UNIQUE SELLING POINT

What is your USP? *Why* do people buy *your* product or service, not somebody else's, what is your plus point? Identify it and build on it, do not destroy it!

Remember, you are selling *benefits*, not products; it can be status, entertainment, enjoyment, attractiveness or convenience just as much as nourishment, or protection or decency. Remember the clothes you are wearing!

SOME RULES FOR SUCCESSFUL MARKETING

o Good marketers sell products that do not come back, to customers who do.

o Successful marketing is a matter of building and sustaining human relationships.

o Put yourself in your customers' shoes.

o Make it easy for people to do business with you.

Personal selling

PREPARATION 1. *To prepare this session you need a cassette recorder, a cassette and at least one person in addition to yourself to tape the dialogues.*

You may prefer to ask three participants to play the roles of George, Carol and Anita (change these names to more familiar ones).

2. *Prepare one copy of Some Tips on Personal Selling for each participant.*

DURATION   *90 minutes*

NOTE: Do not depend on technology (cassette recorder, photocopier and so on). If they are available and work properly, use them. If not, do not just drop this session. Ask some of your participants to do short role-plays simulating situations similar to those in the attached dialogues. There will always be women in a group who like to act. But make sure that the performances are analysed and discussed in such a way that the objective of this session is achieved.

SESSION GUIDE

1. Tell participants that the objective of this session is to enable them to obtain orders from customers in face-to-face selling situations.

2. Ask participants to recall the last time they bought something, whether it was an important purchase or something as insignificant as a cup of tea.

When they actually made the decision, were they on their own or was another person involved, who SOLD them the item?

In almost every purchase decision, the final and the most important part of the marketing process is the personal selling task. This is even more important for the new and small business than for the large corporation whose sales representatives are backed by advertising, a well-known brand and so on.

3. Tell participants that they are about to hear a recording (or observe a role-play) of a sales call by a woman trying to sell dresses to a shop. They should listen carefully and note down every mistake they notice that the woman makes.

4. Play the tape, and if necessary repeat it. Ask a participant to describe the first mistake she heard, and carry on through the dialogue, eliciting at least the following sales errors:

   ○ She forgot the name of the buyer on whom she was calling.

   ○ She had no clear objective for the call, and implied that it was not important.

   ○ She talked about the way in which the product was produced, not its sales advantages, she was 'production oriented' not 'marketing oriented'.

85

- She implied that her own earlier products were no good.
- She did not have full information on her own sales to that customer.
- She only had one type of design, and would not offer anything else.
- She had no samples.
- She criticized what the buyer already had in stock.
- She was not well-informed about the customer's business.
- She offered large discounts as the main sales inducement, suggesting that she had at first tried to 'cheat' this customer.
- She blamed the suppliers and her own employee, rather than taking responsibility herself.
- She was ignorant about her product.
- She allowed herself to be put off and made no attempt to 'close' the sale.

5. Ask participants to recall similar instances when they made the same mistakes, or others; discuss these, and elicit a list of guidelines for positive action when selling, as the opposites of the mistakes made by Carol.

6. Tell participants they are now to hear a tape of Anita selling to the same man. In this case, the tape will be stopped each time George makes an objection, and participants will have to suggest how they would respond.

7. Play through the second dialogue, stopping the tape at each 'pause'; invite participants to suggest their own answers; they plan the next stage, and so on.

8. Ask participants to mention other objections which buyers have brought forward to their products; invite others to suggest how these might be overcome, and remind participants that one mark of an enterprising woman is that she treats problems, such as customer objections, as opportunities.

Tape Dialogue – Selling The Dresses 1

Carol has bought a new sewing machine and has employed a tailor to make a new range of children's dresses; now she has called on Mr George, the garment buyer in Luckys, a department store in town:

Carol: Good afternoon, Mr . . . uh . . . uh . . . uh

George: George is my name.

Carol: Oh yes, Mr George, I happened to be in town this afternoon, so I thought I would drop in as I was passing your shop.

George: Well, it's nice to see you, do sit down. What can I do for you?

Carol: Well, as I said, I was just passing, and I wondered if you might be interested in buying some of the new children's dresses I have started making. They are the very latest designs, and I have got one of the new special electronic tension control sewing machines. The new dresses will sell much better than the ones you have been buying from me, I am sure of that.

George: Well, we are always interested in the latest things; can I have a look at the new range?

Carol: Uh . . . Uh . . . Uh . . . Well, I didn't bring any with me, but they are the latest thing. My cousin brought the designs with her when she came back from London last week.

George: I see, well I seem to remember that the children's dresses you sold me a few weeks ago have not sold very well; how many have we bought from you in the last three months? We could certainly do with something that would sell faster.

Carol: I am not sure what you have been buying, or how many, but I can find out from my books this evening when I go home, and let you know.

George: I see, well, tell me a bit more about the new clothes, for instance, what colours do you have in girls' dresses, and what are the prices?

Carol: I only do pink with white trim, that is what people like, and the selling price is about fifteen dollars each. I am sure you will agree that is good value when you see them.

George: What? That is far too much! Look, this dress sells for ten dollars and lots of our customers say even that is too much.

Carol: My things are much better than that rubbish, and I am sure that with all your branches you could sell lots and lots of my new dresses.

George: Actually, we only have one branch, this one in fact.

Carol: Oh, I must have been thinking of that other company, with all those modern branches in every town. But you need not worry about the price, I can give you a very good discount, maybe ten or twenty per cent off for a decent order.

George: Well, I could think about it, but what about the colours? Some of the

TAPE DIALOGUE – SELLING THE DRESSES 1 (continued)

people who did buy your dresses were complaining about the dyes in your material. They said that the dresses faded after the first washing.

Carol: That is a problem, I know. So many of these ignorant women do not know how to wash clothes properly nowadays, and the textile mills make rubbish; the last tailor I had was a bit of a fool, too, he did not always use the cloth I asked him to, it is so hard to hire sensible people these days.

George: Yes, common sense is very rare. What do you think of this new pre-shrunk cloth that everyone is using? Have you tried it, and do you think it will do what the manufacturers claim?

Carol: Oh, I don't know anything about it, you should ask the representative from the mill. I think.

George: I see. Well, it has been nice talking to you, please come in again when you have something new to show me.

Carol: Thank you, I shall do my best. Good bye, Mr uh . . . uh . . . uh. . . uh. . . .

Tape Dialogue – Selling The Dresses 2

Anita has just started making a new range of children's dresses, and has called on Mr George.

Anita: Good afternoon, Mr George, I called to show you the new range of dresses I have just introduced.

George: I am sorry, it is good of you to call in, but I am very busy and we are really quite happy with our present suppliers of children's dresses.

pause

Anita: I am pleased to hear that, you do have a very attractive display; price, quality, deliveries, they are all perfect, exactly as you ask, are they?

George: Well, I am not sure we always get them exactly when we want them, but really, you are wasting your time; look at the shelves, full of dresses.

pause

Anita: It is a beautiful range, excellently displayed if I may say. But have your customers seen the new style with embroidered fronts? They are all the rage in London I understand.

George: No, I have not come across those; can you show me a sample?

Anita: Yes, of course, here are three different designs, and I can offer the same designs in four different colours.

George: They are attractive, but I suppose they are very expensive too. What do they cost, anyway?

Anita: The cost is fifteen dollars each.

George: What, that is far too much! Our present range average about ten dollars, and many of our customers even complain about that!

pause

Anita: These embroidered dresses really are something different, and I am sure that your class of customers are not only looking for the cheapest things.

George: Well, we try to offer the best designs in town, but fifteen dollars is a bit much, how about a trial order for a dozen dresses at twelve dollars?

pause

Anita: No, Mr George, I am confident that people will be willing to pay extra for a product of this quality, and I operate on a fixed price basis. My prices are fair, and I keep to them.

George: That does make life easier for us too, but these really are a novelty. How can we expect to sell something like this which people have never seen before? If they do notice the dresses in the shop they will not realize that the patterns are embroidered; they will think they are just stuck on.

pause

Anita: Yes, it is difficult, and that is why the firm that made the new embroidery sewing machine has produced this poster with coloured pictures and an

89

TAPE DIALOGUE – SELLING THE DRESSES 2 (continued)

explanation about it. I could let you have several copies of this, along with a couple of sample patterns so that your customers can handle them without soiling the dresses.

George: That's a good idea, but I know what will happen, it is always the same with you women. If the goods sell, we shall not be able to get any more quickly enough, and I daren't order a large quantity without a trial.

pause

Anita: Do not prejudge me; how about that trial order of a dozen you mentioned earlier, and if they go well I can guarantee a further dozen at least twice a week, so long as we have two days' notice.

George: Well, if you could keep to that it would be fine, but look at the time, I really must get back to work. Could you come back next week sometime, so we can talk this over properly?

pause

Anita: I have a full programme next week, and I am sure you want to be among the first to offer these dresses. Make a trial order, and you will be on to a really profitable line.

George: It is tempting, but we just have not got the cash right now, how about letting us have them on sale or return, we will pay when we sell them?

pause

Anita: I am sorry, Mr George, my terms, like my prices, are fair and firm. Cash on delivery, like I do for everyone.

George: You are a hard bargainer, but the manager really has to approve purchases of new lines, you know; could you come back and see him tomorrow morning?

pause

Anita: Mr George, I know you really run this shop, and you do a good job, too. To your customers, these are something new and exciting, and to your shop they will be a new profit earner, but they are still children's dresses, not a new line. Look, let me write out the order on my pad, do you want one of each colour and design, or two of each of the larger ones, or two of each of the smaller ones?

George: Uh . . . uh . . . I am not really sure, but wait a minute, I shall sell a dozen in an afternoon; what about two dozen, so I can have two of each?

pause

Anita: Well, I do have other commitments, but I can manage twenty four for tomorrow afternoon, I shall deliver them myself, along with the posters; shall I come at three thirty or at two?

TAPE DIALOGUE – SELLING THE DRESSES 2 (continued)

George: Come at two, and maybe I can talk about another order if you come the next afternoon, when we see how they have sold.

Anita: Thank you very much, I shall be here promptly at two tomorrow, and if you like I can have a chat with your sales staff so that they can explain the dresses to their customers.

George: By all means, thank you, and good afternoon.

Anita: Thank you, too. Good bye, Mr George.

Some Tips on Personal Selling

Personal face-to-face selling is the 'cutting edge' of marketing, make sure it cuts where and how you want it:

- ○ Prepare for each sales call, have an objective, and know all about the customer and her business with you.

- ○ Make your customer feel important, build her up, do not criticize the competitors' products she has bought before, she decided to buy them, and 'the customer is always right'.

- ○ Be marketing-oriented, not production-oriented, talk about the benefits of the product to your customer, and to her customers if she is going to re-sell your goods, not about how clever you are to produce the goods.

- ○ Offer what the customer wants, not what you find easy to provide.

- ○ Always know all about your product, and carry samples if you can.

- ○ Sell on quality; price reductions imply that you were asking too much at the beginning, and that your quality is not good.

- ○ Take responsibility yourself when things go wrong, don't blame your suppliers, your staff or your customers.

- ○ Listen to the customer, elicit her objections, and deal with them.

- ○ Do all you can to *close* the sale, do not take 'no' for an answer.

Basic business records

PREPARATION

1. *Prepare one copy each of the following exercises for each participant*
   - ○ *'Miss Smith's Cash Book'*
   - ○ *'Jane's Money'*
   - ○ *'Mrs William's Credit Sales'*

2. *Prepare one copy of the handout 'Business Records' for each participant.*

   (Do not forget to change the names into more familiar ones, and the currency into your own currency).

DURATION

315 minutes

SESSION GUIDE

1. Tell participants that the objective of this session is to enable them to identify their needs for business records and to decide what records they should keep.

2. Many participants may have come on the course because they want to know how to keep better business records; stress that keeping records in itself is a waste of time; records must be USED, and the benefits from using them must outweigh the costs of keeping them.

   Ask participants to suggest some of the costs of keeping records; elicit items such as:

   - ○ the paper and pens

   - ○ the tax collector may use them to demand higher taxes

   - ○ family members may demand the profits

   - ○ employees can demand higher wages

   - ○ the time that is spent writing them

   - ○ the time spent learning how to write them

   Stress that business records are an investment of time and money, like any other form of spending; the benefits must outweigh the costs.

3. Ask participants to recall examples of rich and successful businesspeople whom they know, particularly rural and older people, who are often very wealthy indeed. How many of them keep records, or are even literate?

   This shows that records are not a *necessary* condition of business success, and they are certainly not a *sufficient* condition; it can be useful and profitable to keep records, but only if you know how to *use* them, and you *do* use them.

Stress this point yet more by asking some of the older and more established businesswomen in the group to describe what records they keep; they may have none, or they may pay an accountant to keep records for official purposes, but make no use of them themselves.

Stress that you are not suggesting that records should *not* be kept, but only that they should be kept for the right reasons.

4. Ask participants to write down as many reasons as they can why a business such as theirs should have records; elicit suggestions from around the class to include the following:

   ○ to conform to tax laws

   ○ to avoid theft

   ○ to know how much profit you are making

   ○ to calculate prices

   ○ to know when you will be able to afford new equipment

   ○ to keep track of what you owe

   ○ to keep track of what you are owed

   ○ to be sure what money belongs to the business

   Go through each example, and ask participants to suggest ways in which the same objective could be achieved without keeping records; if they cannot do this, remind them that they are many businesspeople who are illiterate; how do they do these things?

   Elicit suggestions such as:

   ○ put money in separate boxes

   ○ make customers record their own transactions in separate books

   ○ do not give or take credit

   ○ handle all money yourself, and count it daily

   ○ only take a fixed sum from the business for yourself each day.

5. Stress that there are no standard 'right' ways to keep records; every businessperson has to decide what is right for herself.

   Choose four or five of the objectives of records already listed. Divide participants into four or five groups, and allocate one objective to each group. Ask the members of each group to work individually on their objective for about ten minutes, and to lay out, on their own, what sort of record they would keep for that purpose.

6. Then ask the members of the groups to come together and to compare what they have done, and then to evolve an agreed approach between them. Warn them that they will have to appoint a spokeswoman who will be responsible for describing their suggestion to the rest of the group.

Allow some 20 or 30 minutes for this; then reconvene the group and ask the spokeswomen for each group to present their answers. Discuss these in turn, and ensure that each record will in fact do what is required.

Do not allow 'experts' to dominate the proceedings, and ensure that everyone understands what is being suggested.

Ensure that participants with differing views have a chance to share their ideas, and that they all appreciate that every business, and every business owner, needs a tailor-made recording system, which must be based on her needs and abilities.

7. Some participants may suggest that it is not necessary for them to keep records, since they can use the services of a bookkeeper or a relative with the necessary skills.

   Ask what problems may arise from this; answers should include:

   o If the owner does not know how to keep the books, how can she supervise whoever does it?

   o The bookkeeper can easily steal the owner's money if the owner does not understand the books.

   o The owner must know how the books are prepared before she can make effective use of them.

   Stress again that records on their own are a cost; it is better not to have them if you do not know how to use them.

8. Distribute the exercise, 'Miss Smith's Cash Book', and allow participants fifteen or twenty minutes to complete it; the objective is to show how important it is to do simple business arithmetic properly, and to appreciate the value of a cash book, *if* it is properly kept.

   Ask participants for their answers; ensure that they recognize that Miss Smith has made two mistakes:

   o she has added $223.40 to $215.60, to make $449 instead of $439

   o she has *added* the $136.80 which was spent on 5 January instead of subtracting it.

   The right balance is therefore $322.20, which is the amount in the cash box; Miss Smith was entirely wrong to dismiss the girl.

9. Distribute 'Jane's Money'; allow about thirty minutes for its completion, and ask participants for their answers: as with the previous exercise, this gives them an opportunity to practise doing simple business arithmetic, and shows how a cash book can help them to keep their own money separate from their business money, which they must do if they are to know how much profit or loss they are making.

   Ask for their answers; if they have added and subtracted correctly, they will have found that the business balance is *nil*. Discuss this finding; show that this does *not* necessarily mean that the business is losing money, because the expenditure includes items such as the deposit on the oven which have not yet been 'used up' in the business.

10. Distribute the exercise, 'Mrs William's Credit Sales', and allow participants at least an hour to complete it; they should not use calculators in this or the previous exercises, even if they are used to doing so at work, because it is vital to be able to do accurate calculations manually; if you make mistakes without a calculator, you will make more and bigger ones with a calculator!

11. Go through their answers; ensure that everyone has laid out a separate account for each customer, and that the figures are neatly presented; when they make mistakes, they should cross out the wrong figure, rather than writing over it, and they should allow plenty of space; paper may be expensive, but it is not as expensive as telling your customers that they owe you less (or more) than they really do.

    The final amounts owing for each customer should be as follows:

✗ Grace – $53.45	Lydia – $75.30	✗ Esther – $51.60
✗ Madeleine – $46.25	✗ Mary – $63.25	✓ Christine – $17.30
✗ Jane –$33.35	✗ Anne –$53.90	Millicent –$50.95
Sarah – $82.30	Emily – $2.65	Katherine – $0.25
Agnes – $14.35	Maureen – $25.00	Kathleen – $60.30

12. When everyone is agreed as to the arithmetic, and the appropriate layout, discuss issues of credit policy:

    o Should they offer credit at all? (Many businesses have to in order to compete; what is important is only to offer credit to the right people, to the right amount, and to record it correctly.)

    o Should the balance be calculated after every transaction? (This is a wise thing to do, so that you can tell at a glance what each credit customer owes, rather than waiting until the end of the month.)

    o How can credit be controlled? (You should only give credit to people you know, and to an agreed limit which is what they can afford.)

    o What should be done when customers delay payment? (Do *not* give any more credit, and use every form of pressure, including the police if necessary, to collect what is owed. It may even be worth spending more on collecting a debt than you actually collect, in order to show people that you mean business.)

✗ wrong amounts see handout.

BUSINESS RECORDS EXERCISE

Miss Smith's Cash Book

Miss Smith kept a small shop, and she employed a young girl to help her serve the customers. Miss Smith went on a traning course and learned how important it is to keep a cash book. As soon as she got home, she started keeping a cash book, and she made sure that she kept it up to date. On the evening of 5 January the cash book looked like this:

DATE	ITEM	CASH IN	CASH OUT	BALANCE
Jan 3	opening balance	—	—	$170.00
	purchase meat	—	$123.45	$46.55
	sales receipts	$229.85	—	$276.40
Jan 4	purchase flour	—	$53.00	$223.40
	sales receipts	$215.60	—	$449.00
	wages	—	$125.00	$324.00
Jan 5	purchase fruit	—	$136.80	$461.20
	sales receipts	$155.00	—	$616.20
	licence	—	$10.00	$606.20

Miss Smith carefully counted the cash in her cash box and found to her great alarm that she only had $322.20.

She immediately sent for the girl, and accused her of theft; she burst into tears and denied the accusation, but Miss Smith dismissed her at once.

QUESTION:

Was Miss Smith right to dismiss the girl as she did?

BUSINESS RECORDS EXERCISE

Jane's Money

Jane realized that she should keep her snack-food business money separate from her personal money, as she had learned at the training course, but she found it very difficult.

She had kept a careful note of all the transactions relating to her business, however, and on 27 January, when she had operated her business since the beginning of the month, the list was as follows:

Jan 3rd	gift from husband	$100.00
	paid deposit for oven	$47.50
	paid for knives and forks	$5.50
Jan 4th	paid for vegetables and fish	$23.50
	paid by Mrs Green for snacks	$10.00
	own cash invested	$16.00
	paid for dishes	$16.00
Jan 7th	paid by George for various goods	$32.00
	paid wage to the helper	$6.00
	paid for flour	$25.00
	taken out for buying school uniform	$11.00
Jan 9th	paid by Mrs Jones for snacks	$12.00
	paid for ingredients	$39.00
	paid for husband's beer	$10.00
Jan 10th	paid for delivered meatballs	$15.00
	paid by Mrs Wright for spring rolls	$5.00
Jan 12th	taken for school fees	$25.00
	paid by Mrs Wright for delivered rolls	$15.00
	paid by Mrs Allen for meatballs	$23.00
	paid for meat	$14.50
	paid for aluminium foil	$5.00
	taken for food	$7.50
Jan 14th	paid wage for helper	$6.00
	payment for oven	$10.00

ASSIGNMENTS:

1. Design a more useful way for Jane to record her cash receipts and payments, and enter these transactions into your new layout.
2. Jane has mixed up her personal cash with the money belonging to the business; how much money should there be in the business?

BUSINESS RECORDS EXERCISE

Mrs Williams' Credit Sales

Mrs Williams runs a small shop in the market, selling groceries. In the middle of January 1991 she started to allow a few of her well-known and trusted customers to buy goods on credit, because some of the other shops were doing this, but she is not happy with the way she records these credit sales, and she is worried about how she will be able to tell her customers what they owe her when they come at the end of the month to pay their bills.

She keeps a careful record of all her credit transactions, but she would like to have a better system than the existing list she keeps. On 26 January the list was as below:

Jan 16th. Grace bought for $34.25
Lydia bought for $10.00
Esther bought for $21.50
Madeleine bought for $13.00
Mary bought for $14.80

Jan 17th. Christine bought for $8.50
Jane bought for $23.90
Anne bought for $18.00
Millicent bought for $9.50

Jan 18th. Esther bought for $32.00
Sarah bought for $5.60
Emily bought for $21.80
Kathleen bought for $3.50
Jane bought for $17.40
Grace bought for $16.00

Jan 19th. Katharine bought for $12.30
Kathleen bought for $8.75
Esther bought for $6.70
Madeleine bought for $29.40

Jan 20th. Christine bought for $13.25
Grace bought for $19.45
Jane bought for $3.25
Kathleen bought for $22.75
Anne bought for $20.90

Jan 21st. Lydia bought for $24.60
Sarah bought for $21.90
Esther bought for $2.55
Madeleine paid $20.00
Millicent bought for $4.70
Emily bought for $25.85
Mary bought for $22.65
Anne paid $10.00
Sarah bought for $20.80

99

BUSINESS RECORDS EXERCISE (continued)

Jan 23rd. Lydia bought for $12.45
           Agnes bought for $14.35
           Jane bought for $8.65
           Millicent bought for £3.85
           Christine bought for $5.55
           Mary bought for $9.65

Jan 24th. Lydia bought for $3.85
           Madeleine bought for $18.55
           Millicent bought for $12.80
           Mary bought for $2.55
           Jane bought for $4.95
           Esther bought for $15.55

Jan 25th. Grace bought for $9.65
           Lydia bought for $8.95
           Maureen bought for $25.00
           Grace paid $20.00
           Madeleine bought for $15.30
           Anne paid $25.00

Jan 26th. Millicent bought for $12.55
           Christine paid $10.00
           Kathleen bought for $11.70
           Katharine bought for $2.95
           Emily paid $10.00
           Sarah bought for $21.65
           Jane paid $30.00

Jan 27th. Esther paid $20.00
           Katharine paid $15.00
           Mary bought for $5.55
           Lydia bought for $15.45
           Jane paid $25.00
           Grace bought for $13.40
           Madeleine paid $45.00

Jan 28th. Christine paid $17.30
           Kathleen bought for $13.60
           Grace paid $75.00
           Mary bought for $7.85
           Madeleine paid $10.00
           Sarah bought for $12.35
           Millicent bought for $7.55
           Emily paid $35.00

ASSIGNMENT:
Design a more useful layout for Mrs Williams' record of what her customers owe her, and make the necessary entries and calculations so that Mrs Williams will have the information she needs.

Business Records

Bookkeeping and accounts are an *investment*, of your time and energy, which must earn a return in terms of improved profit.

Some very successful businesspeople do not keep any records at all; records alone cannot guarantee success.

- If you cannot *use* your business records, don't bother to keep them!

- Every record must have a *purpose; why* do you need that information, how does it help you run your business better?

The most basic records, which even a small business can use, are:

1. THE CASH BOOK: which can be laid out like this:

DATE	ITEM	CASH IN	CASH OUT	BALANCE
....	A description or a reference to an invoice or receipt no.	....	....	....

2. THE BANK BOOK (if you have a bank account): laid out as above, but relating to cheques paid out and received.

3. THE ACCOUNTS RECEIVABLE OR DEBTORS RECORD, which can be laid out thus:

DATE	ITEM	CREDIT GIVEN	CASH PAID	BALANCE
.....	A description or a reference to an invoice or receipt no.	.....	.....	.....

4. THE ACCOUNTS PAYABLE OR CREDITORS RECORD, which can be laid out as below, or can be combined with the Accounts Receivable Record, showing what you owe and what other people owe you.

DATE	ITEM	CREDIT TAKEN	CASH PAID	BALANCE
.....	.....	.....	.....	.....

5. A RECEIPT BOOK: this may be combined with an invoice book, and should have at least two copies, one for the customer or supplier, and one for you to transfer into the Cash Book, the Accounts Receivable or the Accounts Payable Record.

BUSINESS RECORDS EXERCISE (continued)

It should contain the date, the name of the customer or supplier, space for a brief description, a number and space for a signature.

There are many other records which you can have, but with these five you can control your money from day to day, and prepare profit and loss statements and a balance sheet when you need them.

KEEP YOUR RECORDS UP TO DATE!
MAKE SURE THE ARITHMETIC IS RIGHT!

Cash flow

PREPARATION

1. *Prepare copies of the 'Pioneers' Poultry Project' exercise for all participants.*

2. *Prepare copies of the handout The Cash Flow Forecast for all participants.*

DURATION

180 minutes

SESSION GUIDE

1. The objective of this session is to enable participants to prepare a cash flow forecast and to identify its importance for planning their business.

2. Present participants with the following forecast data for *Pauline's Pickle Business*, and ask them to calculate whether it is a viable business or not:

   o estimated sales: 50 jars per month at $4.00 each
   o required monthly wage for Pamela: $50.00
   o empty jars: $0.40 each
   o pickle ingredients: $0.60 per jar

3. Allow participants up to ten minutes to estimate the forecast monthly profit or loss; elicit the following figures:

   o sales: $4.00 x 50 = $200.00 per month
   o Costs:
     labour: $50.00
     empty jars: $0.40 x 50 = $20.00
     ingredients: $0.60 x 50 = $30.00
     Total costs: $100.00
   o Profit: $100.00 per month.

   Clearly this is a viable business; ask participants what further information they would need if they were proposing to set up such a business.

4. Elicit the response that some equipment may be required; tell them that Pauline needs $200.00 worth of equipment, which can be expected to last indefinitely, and that she has $100.00 in cash at her disposal; ask participants how much extra money Pauline will need to borrow in order to be able to start her business.

   Elicit the response that she will need $100.00 in addition to her own $100.00 in order to make the total $200.00 she needs to buy the equipment.

5. Ask participants whether there is any other information they will need before deciding whether or not Pauline should set up this business, and how much capital she will need to do so; participants may suggest that she should be sure that she can make pickles of the necessary quality, she should check that she will in fact be able to continue selling 50 jars a month at $4.00 and that material supplies will be reliable. Ask participants to assume that all the conditions will

103

be satisfied, and ask if there is any further information that is needed before deciding whether, and how, Pauline can establish this business.

Refer to participants' Enterprise Experiences, if this is part of the course; it is unlikely that many of them will have required any equipment, as opposed to raw materials, and all of them should be profitable; did the owners of the businesses require any initial capital over and above the cost of any equipment that was required?

Elicit the response that most required some initial capital, since materials and other supplies almost invariably have to be bought and paid for before the products can be made or any revenues received from sales.

6. Ask participants whether there is any particular feature of pickle-making, or of selling any goods through normal retail grocery shops, which may lead to a particular demand for money with which to start the business, or 'working capital', as cash which is required for raw materials and customer credit is normally called, as opposed to 'fixed capital' which is the name given to money required for equipment.

Elicit the response that pickles usually take some time to make and have to be kept for several weeks before they can be sold, and that most retail shops pay some time after the goods have been received. Ask participants to calculate how much 'working capital' Pauline will require if the pickles take one month to make, if they have to be kept for a further two months before they can be sold, and if the shopkeepers will not pay for a further month; this means that no cash will be received until the fifth month after she has started the business.

7. Elicit the response that Pauline will need to pay her own wages and for jars and raw material for four months before she can receive any cash; she will therefore need;

4 months' 'working capital'	$400.00
Cost of equipment	$200.00
	$600.00
LESS: Her own capital	$100.00
Total loan needed	$500.00

8. Draw up a simple table on the board to illustrate this conclusion, starting with cash received, and then cash going out, and showing the balance remaining at the end of each month; ask participants to state what figures should be written in each column, and complete the table as over:

CASH FLOW FORECAST FOR PAULINE'S PICKLE BUSINESS
(without loan)

Month	1	2	3	4	5	6	7	8	9	10	11	12
CASH IN:												
Balance from last month	0	–200	–300	–400	–500	–400	–300	–200	–100	0	100	200
Owner's investment	100	0	0	0	0	0	0	0	0	0	0	0
Sales	0	0	0	0	200	200	200	200	200	200	200	200
TOTAL IN	100	–200	–300	–400	–300	–200	–100	0	100	200	300	400
CASH OUT:												
Equipment	200	0	0	0	0	0	0	0	0	0	0	0
Materials	50	50	50	50	50	50	50	50	50	50	50	50
Owner's wage	50	50	50	50	50	50	50	50	50	50	50	50
TOTAL OUT	300	100	100	100	100	100	100	100	100	100	100	100
BALANCE	–200	–300	–400	–500	–400	–300	–200	–100	0	100	200	300

Ensure that all participants understand that this shows that if Pauline only has her initial capital of $100.00, she will have a negative balance of $500.00 at the end of the fourth month, and will only reach a positive cash balance after a further five months, that is nine months after starting her business.

Elicit from participants the conclusion that this means she will have to borrow at least $500.00 in order to be able to start her business, and that she will not be able to repay the complete amount until she has been in business for ten months; elicit through discussion the conclusion that she should probably borrow rather more than $500.00, to allow for delays in payment or other unexpected problems, and that a loan of say $600.00, repayable in seven monthly instalments of $100.00 each from month five to month eleven, totalling $700.00 for the loan of $600.00 and interest of $100.00, would probably be arpropriate.

The interest payment will, of course, depend on the rate charged by the lender, this figure of $100.00 for a $600.00 loan for eleven months has been used for the sake of simplicity in calculations.

Stress how different this conclusion is from the suggestion that she would only nccd $100.00 to start her business because she already had $100.00 and the equipment required cost $200.00.

9. Revise the table on the board by adding the loan and the repayments, as shown opposite:

CASH FLOW FORECAST FOR PAULINE'S PICKLE BUSINESS
(with loan)

Month	1	2	3	4	5	6	7	8	9	10	11	12
CASH IN:												
Balance from last month	0	400	300	200	100	100	100	100	100	100	100	100
Owner's investment	100	0	0	0	0	0	0	0	0	0	0	0
Loan	600											
Sales	0	0	0	0	200	200	200	200	200	200	200	200
TOTAL IN	700	400	300	200	300	200	−100	0	100	200	300	400
CASH OUT:												
Equipment	200	0	0	0	0	0	0	0	0	0	0	0
Materials	50	50	50	50	50	50	50	50	50	50	50	50
Owner's wage	50	50	50	50	50	50	50	50	50	50	50	50
Loan repay.					100	100	100	100	100	100	100	
TOTAL OUT	300	100	100	100	200	200	200	200	200	200	200	100
BALANCE	400	300	200	100	100	100	100	100	100	100	100	200

10. Stress that more businesses fail through running-out of 'working capital', because they have not made calculations such as the participants have just completed for Pauline, than fail because of lack of profits; ask participants to give examples from their own business experience of situations when they have been unable to buy as much raw material as they would have liked, not because of shortages, or because of lack of demand, but because they have lacked the cash necessary to continue their businesses at the scale the market warranted.

11. Distribute copies of the exercise 'The Pioneers' Poultry Project' and ask participants to attempt to estimate how much capital the women will need in addition to the $300.00 which they already have. If possible, participants should have at least half an hour to work on this exercise, and if possible the session should be divided into two parts so that they can have time to work on it alone or in groups.

12. Reconvene the participants, and ask them to suggest their solutions to the exercise. Elicit not only their answers, but the method they have used to calculate them, and show that the method you have previously demonstrated for Pauline's Pickle Business is one effective way of working out cash needs. Draw the following table on the board, showing that the same principles apply:

CASH FLOW FORECAST FOR THE PIONEER POULTRY BUSINESS

Month	1	2	3	4	5	6	7	8	9	10	11	12
CASH IN:												
Balance from last month	0	–280	–550	–820	0	–270	–540	280	10	–260	570	300
Members' investment	300	0	0	0	0	0	0	0	0	0	0	0
Sales	0	0	0	1200	0	0	1200	0	0	1200	0	0
TOTAL IN	300	–280	–550	380	0	–270	660	280	10	940	570	300
CASH OUT:												
Shed	200	0	0	0	0	0	0	0	0	0	0	0
Chicks	110	0	0	110	0	0	110	0	0	110	0	0
Feed/Vet	220	220	220	220	220	220	220	220	220	220	220	220
Members' wage	50	50	50	50	50	50	50	50	50	50	50	50
TOTAL OUT	580	270	270	380	270	270	380	270	270	380	270	270
BALANCE	–280	–550	–820	0	–270	–540	280	10	–260	570	300	30

13. Some participants will probably have made similar calculations; ensure that all understand the method, and the implications, namely that:

   o The women will need an additional $820.00 at least, and should try to get $1000.00 to allow for unexpected problems such as higher than normal mortality, delayed payments and so on.

   o If they have to borrow the money, the repayment schedule will have to take account of the cycle of production and cash flow.

   o The women should not withdraw any of the profits for at least one year, since the business will not be making a 'positive cash flow' before that.

   Remind participants of Pauline's Pickle Business; the poultry business is similar in that it is profitable, but needs a large cash input at the beginning. How many participants' businesses or proposed businesses are similarly 'cash hungry'?

14. Point out that bank managers or lending institutions will require calculations of this type in order to show what loan is needed and how it can be repaid; stress that a prospective borrower is far more likely to be able to obtain the funds she needs if she is able to present an estimate of her future cash flows in this form, together with a suggestion of the amount she will need to borrow and how it can be repaid.

   Point out that all participants should try to make calculations of this type for the future of their own businesses, whether or not they require loans, in order to ensure that they are using their cash as effectively as possible and that they will be able to finance any ideas they may have for expansion; the cash flow forecast is possibly the most important part of the business planning process which they are all to go through.

CASH FLOW EXERCISE

The Pioneers' Poultry Project

The Young Pioneers, a women's group, decided that they would start a broiler chicken business, since they knew that there was a good demand for chicken meat from local hotels and schools, and they wanted to increase their incomes. They agreed that they would share the work of raising the chickens, and that members would be paid according to how many hours they worked. They agreed to share the surplus, if any, after each cycle of chicken production, and to start a new cycle immediately after each batch had been sold, in order to provide themselves with a continuous income.

They had saved $200.00 from their fund raising activities, and each of the ten members was willing to invest a further $10.00 in the new venture. They wanted to know if this would be enough, and, if not, how much more money they would need to borrow, and for how long.

They had obtained the following information:

Cost of chicken shed	$200.00
Cost of day old chicks, 220 at 50 cents each	$110.00
Feed and veterinary care, $1.00 per chick per month	
Women's wages, $50.00 per month	
Time taken for chicks to reach maturity	3 months
Selling price per mature bird	$6.00
Probable mortality, 20 birds, leaving 200 to be sold.	

ASSIGNMENT:

1. Calculate how much extra capital the Young Pioneers will need in order to start and run their business successfully.

2. Assuming that the business goes according to plan, how much of the profits would you recommend that the members should distribute after each cycle?

The Cash Flow Forecast

You should always prepare a Cash Flow Forecast whenever you want to start a new business or expand or change an existing one; it will help you to avoid running out of cash, and to calculate how much money you need to raise, from a bank or elsewhere, *before* you undertake any new venture.

To forecast your cash flows, you need to know the *amount* of cash that will be 'flowing' into and out of the business, and *when* it will be 'flowing'. Even if your costs are much lower than your sales, so that you are making a good *profit*, you can still 'go broke' because you have allowed your customers too much credit, or have underestimated the time it takes to produce your goods.

The forecast can be laid out as follows:

	Month 1	Month 2	Month 3	Month 4	Month 5	Month 6 etc.
CASH IN						
Balance	nil	−1600	−3200	−4800	−2400	nil
Capital	1000					
Loans	nil					
Sales	nil	nil	nil	4000	4000	4000
TOTAL IN	1000	−1600	−3200	−800	1600	4000
CASH OUT						
Equipment	1000					
Wages	500	500	500	500	500	500
Materials	400	400	400	400	400	400
Salary	600	600	600	600	600	600
Other	100	100	100	100	100	100
TOTAL	2600	1600	1600	1600	1600	1600
BALANCE	−1600	−3200	−4800	−2400	nil	2400

The example shows that even a business with monthly profits of $2400 (sales $4000 – costs $1600), and when the owner has enough capital to buy equipment ($1000) will need a loan of over $4800 if the time taken between starting production and receiving payment is three months, which is quite normal.

The profit and loss account

PREPARATION   *Prepare copies of the handout 'The Profit and Loss Account' for all participants.*

DURATION   *135 minutes*

NOTE: If you have experience of formal accountancy or book-keeping you may feel that this and the subsequent session on the Balance Sheet are over-simplified. You should nevertheless try to forget what you know about debits and credits and so on; the approach in these sessions has been used successfully many times, all over the world, to enable businessmen and businesswomen for the first time actually to understand and *use* financial accounts in order to make more effective use of their resources.

SESSION GUIDE

1. Tell participants that the objective of this session is to enable them to produce and use a profit and loss account.

2. Ask a participant who is already in business, but is unlikely to be keeping complete records of revenues and costs, whether she does, in fact, know on a regular basis how much money her business is making or losing. When you have identified someone who does not, state that the class will now produce a 'profit and loss account' for her business, which will be at least as accurate as her memory for a few vital facts.

   In the unlikely event that all the participants who are already in business have up-to-date profit and loss accounts, ask one to answer the following questions in terms of the present month or any other recent period for which the accounts have not yet been prepared.

   If none of the participants are yet in business, you have three options:

   ○ ask a participant to give the required information for her Enterprise Experience business as it stands today; or

   ○ ask a participant to give the best guesses she can for a business with which she is familiar, such as one belonging to a relative or friend, or one where she regularly makes purchases; or

   ○ ask a participant to use her imagination, and to give reasonable answers for any kind of business she prefers to use.

3. Ask the chosen participant how much her sales amounted to in the last complete month; she may find it difficult to remember, but elicit from other participants suggestions as to how an approximate figure can be arrived at even if no records have been kept and the owner does not remember the total of sales in money terms; elicit suggestions such as:

111

○ the average number of meals, dresses, chickens, eggs, or whatever the products are which were sold each day, week or month, times the average price charged for each.

○ if the owner cannot remember the above, the total amount of raw materials used, such as sacks of flour, metres of cloth or bags of cement, converted into the expected number of products this would allow to be made and sold.

Ensure that both cash and credit sales are included, and that cash received for credit sales made in previous months is excluded.

Stress that these only give very approximate figures, but such figures are better than nothing; remind participants that if they keep a cash book and debtor record as discussed in the earlier session both revenue and money spent can be easily extracted from the records.

4. Write down the figures for sales in a month, and then elicit the cost of raw materials used in the same way as the figure for sales revenue. A suggestion on how to lay out the figures of a profit and loss account in a simple way is given on the last page of this session guide.

Ask participants why the amount of money spent on raw materials in a month may not be the right figure to use for the cost of raw materials used in the month; if necessary, ask participants to think not of a month's sales but one day's sales; why cannot a tailor, for instance, calculate her profit for a day by taking the amount she spent on cloth and other supplies that day from what she sold?

Elicit the response that she probably does not buy cloth every day, and may in fact buy no cloth at all for some days, and then buy enough on one day for far more dresses than she can make in that day; the level of *stocks* of cloth goes up and down, so that the amount of stock *used* is what should be set against the sales, not the amount of cloth *bought* on that particular day. Show that this is why the Cash Flow is different from the Profit and Loss.

5. Ask the participant whose results are being used as an example whether her stocks of materials are always more or less the same at the start and at the end of each month; if they are, and are always likely to be, it may be reasonable to use the amount *spent* as the amount *used*; in most businesses, except those with very perishable products which have to be sold each day, the stocks vary from one period to another.

Ask participants to suggest how the amount *used* can be calculated, if the amount purchased, and the amount in stock at the beginning and at the end are known; show, if necessary by using stick of chalk or other items as a demonstration, how the calculation is done:

amount USED in a period
equals
amount in stock at start
plus
amount added to stock during period
less
amount in stock at end of period.

6. Stress that the actual amounts in stock must be counted at the end of each period for an accurate calculation of the profit or loss. Discuss the various approaches to stock-taking in various types of business; stress that it is necessary not only for calculating profit or loss, but also to find out if there has been any pilfering, to throw out damaged stock and to ensure that everything is in good order.

7. Ask the chosen participant for her estimates of stock at the beginning and end of the month she is describing, and for the amount purchased; carry out the calculation as above, and take the result from the revenue.

   Show that this is the 'Gross margin' or 'Gross profit' for the period; ask the participants what other expenses she had during the period. Elicit, if necessary by asking others to suggest what has been omitted, items such as:

   ○ Wages paid to any employees.

   ○ Wages or salary paid by the owner to herself. (Stress that this is often omitted, and discuss the problems that may arise when a one-woman business, where no charge has been made for the owner's wages, expands and employs others; there is a sudden increase in costs which may destroy the basis on which goods have been priced and sold.)

   ○ Rent, electricity, water, licences.

   ○ Maintenance of equipment.

   ○ Any supplies such as stationery, lubricants or other items which are used but not directly related to production like cloth, flour or timber.

   ○ Some allowance for the cost of replacement of equipment; remind participants about the concept of depreciation which was introduced in the ealier session on Costing and Pricing; explain this and show how both inflation and changes in equipment designs make this of little use as a way of actually ensuring that a business has enough money to buy new equipment when it is needed, but show that some allowance is needed for this cost.

   ○ Any other cost items such as interest payments, taxes, or transport charges for goods or people.

8. Take the total of these other items from the 'gross margin' to show the actual profit or loss. Ask the participant to state whether this is higher or lower than she expected; ask her, and others, to suggest how this information might be used to improve the profitability of the business and elicit suggestions such as:

   ○ To compare performance from one period with another, in order to see whether progress is being made.

   ○ To relate various costs to sales revenue and to one another, such as materials to revenue, wages to revenue, materials to transport costs and others as participants may suggest.

   ○ To help the owner to decide whether she and/or other owners should make any withdrawals from the business, in addition to whatever wages or salary she is drawing.

     ○ To help calculate costs and thus to set prices.

9. Ask the participant whose business is being used as an example if she sells more than one product. If she only sells one standard item, identify a participant who sells several different items. Ask her, and the other participants, whether a profit and loss account for such a business shows which products are more or less profitable. Clearly it does not, since all the costs and the sales are added together.

10. Show by eliciting examples from participants that many businesswomen fail to realize that some of their products may be losing money while others are profitable. Ask particpants why this is *sometimes* good business, *so long as the owner knows that she is doing it*:

     ○ it may be necessary to attract customers by bargains, so that they will then buy more profitable goods in addition.

     ○ some unprofitable goods, such as price-controlled items, may have to be offered in order to make up a complete range.

Refer back to the session on Costing and Pricing; stress that every business-woman must know how much profit (or loss) her whole business is making *and* how much each product or service she sells is contributing to the total result.

11. If time allows, go through one or more participants' figures in the same way, allowing other participants to ask the questions so that all are aware of the questions that must be asked.

12. Suggestion for the lay-out of a simple Profit and Loss Account (see over):

PROFIT AND LOSS ACCOUNT FOR APRIL 1991

Sales		$500
less Costs:		
opening stocks	$100	
plus purchases	50	
less stocks at the end of the period	70	
	———	
equal stocks used during the period		$80
		———
Gross margin or gross profit		$420
less Other Expenses:		
. wages	$100	
. rent	50	
. supplies	20	
. depreciation	50	
. transport	10	
. payment of interests on loan, taxes	10	
	———	
		$240
		———
Net Profit		$180
		═══

The Profit and Loss Account

The Profit and Loss Account is a statement of the income and the expenditure of a business over a period; the business owner should decide for herself how frequently she needs to produce it.

EARNINGS, NOT CASH:

The income includes amounts which have been earned but have not yet been paid for, and items which have been used, whether they were paid for during, before or after the period, because they were bought or sold on credit. The Cash Flow statement shows how the *cash* moves, while the Profit and Loss shows what has been *earned* and *used*.

THE USE OF EQUIPMENT:

The cost of 'wear and tear' on equipment is shown by *depreciation*; the amount is calculated by dividing the cost of the equipment by the years it will last, and including the resulting amount as the cost of using that equipment for a year. Remember, inflation means that the amount included for depreciation will hardly ever be enough to pay for new equipment.

THE AMOUNT OF STOCKS USED:

The *purchases* of stocks during a period are not usually the same as the amount *used*, because the stocks at the beginning and the end of the period are not usually the same; the amount *used* is calculated as follows:

Stocks at the beginning of the period
PLUS
Stocks purchased during the period
LESS
Stocks remaining at the end of the period
EQUALS
Stocks used during the period

THE PROFIT AND LOSS ACCOUNT (continued)

The Profit and Loss Account is used to find out what profit has been made so that the owner(s) can decide what drawings, if any, they should take out (*but*, remember, it does not show the *cash* available), so the profits may not be available for drawing because they are invested in stocks, equipment or other *assets*.

You can also use it to be sure that important costs such as raw materials or other items are being controlled properly, that prices are not too low, and that sales are growing according to plan.

The following is an example of a simple Profit and Loss Account:

PROFIT AND LOSS ACCOUNT FOR APRIL 1991

Sales		$500
less Costs:		
opening stocks	$100	
plus purchases	50	
less stocks at the end of the period	70	
equals stocks used during the period		$80
Gross margin or gross profit		$420
less Other Expenses:		
. wages	$100	
. rent	50	
. supplies	20	
. depreciation	50	
. transport	10	
. payment of interest on loan, taxes	10	
		$240
Net profit		$180

The balance sheet

PREPARATION   *Prepare copies of the handout 'The Balance Sheet' for all participants.*

DURATION   *135 minutes*

SESSION GUIDE

1. The objective of this session is to enable participants to prepare a balance sheet and use it as a tool for understanding how money is being used in their businesses, and for deciding how it can be used better.

2. Ask if any participant has a balance sheet for her business, whether this is prepared by herself, an accountant or an outside auditor. If anyone does, which is unlikely, ask her how she *uses* the balance sheet to help her manage her business.

   It is even more unlikely that anyone actually does use her balance sheet; stress that very few small or new businesses have balance sheets of any kind, and that very few managers or owners of even quite large businesses actually *use* their balance sheets as management tools, even though the balance sheet is perhaps the most powerful tool for understanding how money is used in a business, and for deciding how it can be used better.

   Ensure that any participant who does have (and maybe even uses) a balance sheet is recognized, and that she attempts to explain it. Stress that accountants often conceal the true value of documents such as a balance sheet from their clients because of the complex language they use. If the Enterprise Experience is part of this course, remind participants of their efforts to present balance sheets for their enterprises; they will now have the opportunity to see how simple a balance sheet really is.

3. A balance sheet is no more than a statement of where the money in a business came from, and how it is being used, at a particular moment in time; the Cash Flow Forecast, as we saw in the earlier sessions, describes how cash will flow into and out of a business over a period, and the Profit and Loss Account shows how much money the business earned (or lost) during a period. The balance sheet is a 'snap shot' of the business at one moment, showing the sources and uses of money at that time.

   If the Enterprise Experience is part of the course, ask a participant whose Enterprise Experience business was financed by the owner(s)' money and by a loan to describe the way the money was used, and where it came from, when they had borrowed the money but had not yet bought any materials or equipment. If the Enterprise Experience is not included, ask a participant to imagine that she is starting a simple trading business.

   For the sake of simplicity at the start, choose an enterprise where the owner(s) did not bring any articles such as things to sell or materials from their own resources, but contributed only money at the beginning.

Elicit figures such as the following, and write them on the board in the following form. Stress that details such as the sequence of the figures, or whether the sources are on the left or the right, are unimportant, and stress also that the terminology is not important; what matters is that they should understand what the balance sheet *means*, and how it can be *used*.

Where the money came from		How the money is used	
Owner(s)	$20	Cash	$50
Loan	$30		
Total	$50	Total	$50

Point out to the participant that she has now produced a balance sheet for her enterprise when it started. Ask other participants to suggest differences in their enterprises, and show how items such as equipment would be included in the 'uses' column, as well as cash, and how their value should be included in the 'sources' column, as part of the owner(s)' investment.

4. Ask the participant to state what happened (or might happen) next in her business. She/they probably bought some materials. Write up a second balance sheet in the following form:

Where the money came from		How the money is used	
Owner(s)	$20	Cash	$10
Loan	$30	Materials	$40
Total	$50	Total	$50

Ensure that all participants appreciate that no new money has gone into or out of the business; the only change is that the ways in which the same amount of money is being used have changed.

5. Ask the same participant to describe how the money is being used now, when the materials have all been processed and sold, and there only remains cash in the business. If none of the Enterprise Experiences have reached this stage, or the Enterprise Experience is not being used, ask them to imagine that the business you are discussing has reached the stage, and to suggest how the money is being used when that point is reached. Elicit figures such as the following:

Where the money came from		How the money is used	
Owner(s)	$20	Cash	$60
Loan	$30		
Total	$50	Total	$60

119

Show that the figures no longer balance; if the cash is correctly calculated, the figures must balance, because a balance sheet is no more than a statement of two things about the same sum of money, there is no miracle to the fact that the figures at the bottom of the columns are the same.

6. Ask participants to suggest what is missing; what is the additional entry in the 'where the money came from' column that must be added to make the totals balance?

   Elicit the answer that the additional money must have come from the 'profits' earned by the business, as a result of selling whatever they made with the materials which have been used up. Elicit similar examples from other Enterprise Experience businesses or participants' own businesses to show how the profit (or loss) is the balancing factor after some sales have been made.

7. Insert the balancing figure as below, and stress that if the enterprise in question had kept a proper record of sales and expenses, through the cash book and the record of credit given or taken, the resulting figure for profit would have been the same as they have now shown to be the case by comparing the balance sheets at the start and at the end of the period. Remind participants that they will have to produce similar balance sheets for their Enterprise Experiences, together with cash books and profit and loss accounts.

Where the money came from		How the money is used	
Owner(s)	$20	Cash	$60
Loan	$30		
Profits	$10		
Total	$60	Total	$60

8. Ask one or more participants who have never prepared balance sheets for their own businesses to give estimates for the ways money is being used in their businesses, such as stocks, equipment, buildings, cash, money owed by customers and bank balances. Ask them, also, for the sources from which the business has received money from outside, such as their own original investment, any other money they have invested later, money owed to suppliers or deposited in advance by customers, or loans outstanding.

   Ensure that all participants understand why each of these items is a use of money, or a place from which money has come; add up the two columns, and show that the balancing figure in the 'sources' column is the accumulated profit, or, if it is a negative amount, the accumulated losses, of the business.

   Many participants may be surprised at the fact that their businesses have accumulated large profits; they should be congratulated, and this is a powerful demonstration of how the balance sheet can show the owner of a business what she did not know before.

The Balance Sheet

A balance sheet is a statement about the money that is in a business; it states how the money is being *used* (the 'assets') and where it came from (the 'liabilities'), at a particular moment in time.

The following example shows a simple balance sheet for a tailoring business:

Balance Sheet for Angela's Tailoring Business, 31/12/90

How the money is used (assets)		Where it came from (liabilities)	
Cash	$100	Accounts payable	$250
Accounts receivable	150	Customer deposits	100
Stocks	500	Bank loan	500
Equipment	1000	Owner's capital	500
Insurance prepaid	100		
	———		———
	$1850		$1350

This shows more uses than sources; if all the other items have been correctly included, the only additional sources must be the PROFITS which Angela has made and has not withdrawn; this is in fact the major source of capital for most small businesses.

Reinvested profits	500
	———
	$1850

If the uses had added up to *less* than the sources, the difference would have been the *losses* which the business had made in the past. If regular and accurate accounts have been kept, the profit or loss will be known, but for many businesses the only way to find out whether it has made money in the past is to total the present uses and sources, and to see whether there is a balancing loss or profit.

A balance sheet such as this shows where the money is being used; the owner can see what she has, and can see, if she needs more stocks for instance, that she can get the money by collecting money owed by her customers, waiting until she has earned more profits, using some of her cash or even by selling some of her equipment if it is not fully used.

The break even point

PREPARATION   *Ensure that all participants have copies of 'Catherine's Dresses', the case study from the session on Costing and Pricing.*

DURATION   *90 minutes*

SESSION GUIDE

1. The objective of this session is to enable participants to estimate the volume of sales at which their businesses will 'break even'; that is neither make a profit nor a loss.

2. Remind participants of the two earlier sessions on the Profit and Loss Account and on Costing and Pricing; refer to the example of 'Catherine's Dresses' and ask participants how much profit she would make if she had sold 50 dresses a month at $10.74 each; elicit the response that she would make no profit or loss, she would earn the $100 wages which was her minimum target, and she would cover the 'fixed' costs of her supplies and the depreciation of the sewing machine, but there would be no allowance for sickness, for selling or purchasing time and in fact the business would barely survive.

3. Ask participants to suggest what Catherine's monthly profit or loss account would look like if she did in fact sell 50 dresses a month at $10.74 each; elicit the following suggestion:

   o Sales: 50 dresses at $10.74 each $537.00

   o Cost of materials (assuming no stock at the beginning
      or at the end of the month): 50 × $8.50 $425.00
                                                                         _____
   o Gross margin: $112.00

   o Other Expenses:
      . Labour: $50.00
      . Supplies: $42.00
      . Depreciation of sewing machine: $6.00
                                            _____
      Total expenses $112.00

   o Profit/loss: nil

4. Remind participants of the earlier session on Costing and Pricing and ask what is basically different about the cost of materials from the other costs; elicit the suggestion that the cost of ingredients varies directly with the number of dresses which are made, whereas Catherine wants to earn $600 however many dresses she makes, the machine will depreciate and the supplies are likely, more or less, to cost the same.

   Show that costs can therefore be roughly divided into 'fixed costs', which

122

remain the same whatever the level of production, and 'variable costs', which vary directly with the amount of goods produced.

Ask participants to suggest what are the fixed and variable costs for their own businesses; discuss issues such as their own labour and wages paid to others, and show that except for casual labour which is recruited and paid day by day, most labour costs, including, in particular, that of the owners themselves, can be regarded as fixed.

5. Ask participants what would be the results of Catherine's business if she was able to charge not $10.74 for each dress but $11.00; allow participants a few minutes to do the calculations and elicit the answer that the business would make a profit of $13.00, or 26 cents for each of the 50 dresses.

6. Ask participants what Catherine should do if she was selling the dresses for $10.74, and thus 'breaking even', and then discovered another customer who would buy the dresses for $11.30 each, rather than $10.74, but would only take 40 dresses a month rather than 50. What would the effect be on Catherine's results?

   Allow participants a few minutes to work out the answer, and elicit the correct solution, namely that she would still 'break even' because each dress would 'earn' $2.80 rather than $2.24, above the cost of materials, and she would therefore be able to cover the costs of her labour, the depreciation of the sewing machine and the supplies by selling fewer dresses at the higher price.

7. Ask participants to work out what would be the result if Catherine's customer insisted on reducing the price per dress to $10.10, but agreed to take 70 dresses per month, and if Catherine found that she could still make this quantity in the same time because she had learned to work faster.

   Elicit the response that she would still 'break even' because each dress would now 'earn' only $1.60, but the higher quanity would compensate for the lower price, since 70 x $1.60 = $112.00, which is Catherine's total 'fixed costs'.

8. Check that participants understand the principle of fixed and variable costs, and the concept of each product 'earning' or 'contributing' a certain amount to cover the fixed costs; elicit examples from participants' own businesses, and make rough calculations of break even points (BEP) and levels of profits which would be achieved at various pricing levels.

9. Ask participants whose businesses or proposed businesses will offer more than one product or service to suggest how they can calculate their BEP; clearly a different approach is needed because the 'contribution' per product is unlikely to be the same.

   Ask participants to suggest a common unit of sales for a multi-product business. Elicit the answer that *money* is the common unit which enables a business owner to express the total of her sales.

   Show that it is possible to calculate an average contribution per dollar as well as per product; ask participants to work out the contribution per dollar of

Catherine's business when she was selling 70 dresses per month at $10.10. Go through the calculation as follows:

- total sales: 70 × $10.10   = $707
- less variable costs 70 × $8.50   = $595

- contribution $112

- contribution per dollar of sales: $112 ÷ $707 = approx. $0.16

She can now estimate her break even point in dollars, as opposed to dresses, by calculating how many units (dollars) each contributing 16 cents ($0.16) will be needed to cover her fixed costs of $112:

- $112 ÷ $0.16 = approx. $700

This calculation is of course unnecessary for Catherine, since she is making only one design of dress.

A businesswoman who sells different products must calculate the average number of cents per dollars (or the average percentage) contributed by her sales to fixed costs, and then see how many dollars of sales she will need to make in order to cover the fixed costs.

Check participants' understanding by asking those with existing or proposed multi-product businesses to apply this approach to estimate their BEP.

10. Ask particpants to suggest how this type of calculation can be of use in their businesses; elicit examples such as:

- To estimate the possible effects on profits of reduction of prices which might increase sales, or increases of prices which might decrease sales.

- To assess the effect on profits of reductions in raw materials or labour costs.

- To assist in making decisions whether to pay other businesspeople to carry out tasks such as transport, finishing, cutting, initial preparation or whatever, thus causing these task to be 'variable costs', but probably reducing profits at the same time.

If time allows, discuss decisions which may be facing participants in their businesses at the present time and show how calculations of the break even point and estimation of the fixed and variable costs and various levels of operation can assist in business decision-making.

Calculating The Break Even Point

The break even point (BEP for short) is the level of sales at which your business will neither make a profit nor a loss; the revenues will be exactly the same as the costs.

It is important to know your BEP because it is a warning that you are very near to losing money, and it helps you to estimate the effects on your profits of higher or lower prices, or higher or lower sales. To calculate the BEP you must first divide your costs into the *variable* costs, which change directly with the amount you sell, and the *fixed* costs, which remain the same even when your sales change.

Variable Costs include:

- cloth for tailors
- feed for a poultry business
- food for a restaurant
- petrol for a taxi

Fixed Costs include:

- wages, unless you pay workers only according to the quantity they produce
- rent, licences, usually water and electricity
- your own salary.

To calculate your BEP:

- Find out how much variable cost is included in the cost of each item.
- Subtract this from the total selling price.
- The remaining amount is the 'contribution' which has to pay for your fixed costs.
- Add up the total of your fixed costs for a month.
- Divide this total by the 'contribution' for each item.
- The result is the number of items which you must sell in a month to pay the variable materials included in each item, *and* the fixed costs.

If you sell more than one type of product, you can estimate your BEP in sales turnover, by dividing the fixed costs by the average percentage contribution for each dollar of sales. The answer will be the turnover figure at which your business breaks even, assuming that the contribution percentage is approximately the same for all your products.

If you are considering changing your selling prices, you can estimate the effect of this on your profits by doing the same set of calculations with different prices and different possible quantities which you think you may sell. This will help you decide which price is most profitable, because a lower price *may* be the most profitable, if you sell enough to pay for the fixed costs, but it may be better to have a higher price, because of the higher contribution this will bring in for each item sold.

Sources and uses of money

PREPARATION   *Prepare copies of the handout 'Where to get money from' for all participants.*

DURATION   *90 minutes*

SESSION GUIDE

1. Tell participants that the objective of this session is to enable them to examine different ways of raising money and identify the 'mix' of sources of finance that is most suitable for their circumstances.

2. Ask participants where businesses get money from; elicit the obvious reply: 'by borrowing it from a bank'.

   Ask whether any of the participants have ever borrowed money from a bank; was it easy, quick and inexpensive?

   Clearly the answer will be 'No'; explain that the objective of this session is to examine other ways of raising money for a business, so that participants can examine each of them and identify the 'mix' of sources of finance that is most suitable for their circumstances.

3. Remind participants that money in itself is of no use; people only want it because they need things which they can buy with money.

   Ask participants to give examples of the things they want to buy, and for which they are trying to obtain funds; elicit examples such as:

   o Raw materials

   o Spare parts

   o Equipment

   o Advance rent etc

   o Premises

   o A vehicle

   Ensure that they also include items such as money to finance credit to customers, which is a use of money in just the same way as stocks or equipment.

4. Ask participants who have borrowed from banks to describe what is involved; elicit the disadvantages of loans of this kind;

   o Interest has to be paid.

   o Security is required.

   o It takes a long time to get a decision.

   o 'Inducements' may have to be given.

   o The repayment schedule is inflexible.

126

5. Ask participants to write down as many different sources of money as they can; they should refer to the list of typical things for which money is needed, since this may remind them of particular sources of finance which are 'tied' to particular items.

After some five or ten minutes, ask each participant in turn to name one source of money, and if necessary to explain it by reference to one of the items previously listed.

Go round the group in turn, until all the possibilities have been listed. The list should include at least the following, and particpants may include others:

o Own savings

o Family money

o Deposits from customers

o Credit (that is, in effect, loans) from suppliers

o Hire-purchase finance

o Profits of the enterprise itself

6. When this list has been completed, ask participants to think about their own businesses; how do they actually raise money, for particular purchases, quite apart from the sources already listed?

If necessary, ask a participant to describe the last time she paid for something for her business; this should not be a new capital purchase, but an ordinary day-to-day purchase. If no participants have actually started their businesses ask them to think about other businesses; where do they get money for their day-to-day purchases?

She, or they, will have paid for it out of her cash or bank balance; ask where this money came from. The answer will be 'from customers' payments'; ask what the customers have paid for; the answer is of course the goods they bought.

Elicit, through discussion, the conclusion that this transaction in fact involves the business obtaining cash, with which to pay for supplies, by converting goods into cash.

7. Stress that the most frequent source of money for a business is in fact the business itself; cash is taken from one use and put to another, as in the example of selling goods in order to pay for supplies.

Ask a participant who is well-established in business to list the 'assets', or ways in which the money she has in her business is being used. Or, if none are yet in business, once again to think about other businesses; how are they using their money? After she has suggested certain headings, ask other participants to suggest others, and list the possibilities as follows:

o Stocks of materials

o Stocks of goods ready for sale

o Goods in the process of being made

○ Cash

○ Equipment and tools

○ Motor vehicles

○ Money owed by customers

○ Buildings

8. Ask participants to suggest ways in which each of the above can be 'converted' into cash, to be used for buying something else; some of the answers are obvious, but others may be more difficult; they should include the following:

○ Material stocks: Turn into goods and sell them, or sell any excess for whatever price it will fetch.

○ Work in progress: Finish off and sell half-made goods, and do not start new goods until bills have been paid.

○ Finished stocks: Sell off, for cash, reducing prices if necessary.

○ Money owed by customers: Sell only for cash, press late payers to settle their accounts.

○ Machines and equipment: Sell off or lease out any under-used machines.

○ Buildings: Sell them, and rent premises instead.

Stress that bankers will not lend money to anyone who is not making the best possible use of what she already has.

9. Relate the answers to the earlier session on the Balance Sheet; remind participants that a balance sheet shows how money is being used in a business, and where it came from. A businesswoman can use her balance sheet to see which 'assets' might be turned into cash, and which 'liabilities', or stocks, can be tapped for more money.

10. Ask participants who claim their businesses need money and who propose to apply for bank loans, to describe what they want to buy; ask them, or others, to suggest alternative ways of raising the finance, resulting from this session; examples might include:

○ Raw materials: customers to buy them, or to make deposits.

○ Equipment: rent from other people, hire purchase.

○ Customers demanding credit: do not give it to them!

○ Cash for a buying trip abroad: exports of local goods, even at a loss.

11. If time allows, and some participants have actual business experience, ask them to describe occasions when they have raised money from inside and from outside their businesses; ask others to describe their needs for finance, and help them to see through sharing their problems with others that they may be able to raise the necessary funds without going outside the business.

Where To Get Money From?

Have you ever borrowed money from a bank? If yes; was it easy, quick and inexpensive? Certainly not! Interest has to be paid, security is required, it takes a long time to get a decision, 'inducements' may have to be given, and the repayment schedule is inflexible.

But there are other sources, and other ways of raising money for your business, for examples:

○ your own savings

○ family money

○ deposits from customers

○ credit (that is, in effect, loans) from suppliers

○ hire-purchase finance

○ profits of the enterprise itself

The most frequent source of money for a business is, in fact, the business itself; cash is taken from one use and put to another, or is earned from profit and re-invested. The ways in which money is used in a business, that is the assets of a business, are for example:

○ stocks of materials

○ stocks of goods ready for sale

○ goods in the process of being made

○ cash

○ equipment and tools

○ motor vehicles

○ money owed by customers

○ buildings

These assets can be converted into cash:

○ Material stocks:	Turn into goods and sell them, or sell any excess for what it will fetch.
○ Work in progress:	Finish off and sell half-made goods, and do not start new goods until bills have been paid.
○ Finished stock:	Sell off, for cash, reducing prices if necessary.
○ Money owed by customers:	Sell only for cash, press late payers to settle their accounts.

WHERE TO GET MONEY FROM? (continued)

○ Machines and equipment: Sell off or lease out any under-used machines.

○ Buildings: Sell them, and rent premises instead.

You should examine each of these possibilities and identify the 'mix' of sources of finance that is most suitable for your circumstances.

Bankers will not lend money to anyone who is not making the best possible use of what she already has.

The Enterprise Experience V

PRESENTATION OF FINAL RESULTS

PREPARATION

1. *About three days before this session distribute copies of the 'Guidelines for the Presentation of the Final Results', and remind participants to have their accounts ready as stated in point 8 of the guidelines.*

2. *Participants may ask for flip chart paper or the like to prepare their presentations; make sure that it is available.*

3. *Collect participants' books and statements at the nominated time on the day before the presentations.*

4. *Invite the 'banker' or another of your colleagues to help you with the assessment of the results and the selection of the winner(s).*

5. *Decide what other prize you want to give in addition to those you have already mentioned during the first session. For example, the most friendly business, or the best presentation, or the best marketing.*

6. *If you are giving a prize for the best-kept books, decide to which business to give it.*

7. *Have the prizes ready for the session.*

DURATION

180 minutes (or more, depending upon the number of enterprises)

SESSION GUIDE

1. The objective of this session is to enable participants to present and compare their enterprise results with one another, and to 'process' the final stages and the whole of the Enterprise Experience.

2. Start the session by asking a representative of each business to repay their loan, if one was made and not yet repaid, together with interest, and to receive back the security offered at the time of borrowing.

   If any enterprises fail to repay their loan, ensure that the security is retained by the 'bank' as was originally stated.

3. A representative from each enterprise should then be given up to ten minutes to present the results of the enterprise, together with the figures, and a very brief statement of why she/they felt they succeeded or failed.

4. For the first time, it should be clear which the 'winning enterprise' is during these presentations, being the one that achieved the highest earnings, in terms of any wages paid and final profit, per owner.

Problems may arise in terms of definition, in that some enterprises may decide not to sell used equipment but to divide it among the owners as wages, while others may intend to sell such equipment but have not yet actually done so. It is important that their results should have been appraised beforehand, to avoid any under or overstatement of profit.

5. After all the enterprise results have been presented, the winner(s) should be announced and suitable prize(s) awarded; this should probably not be in money, but should be a modest, but nevertheless very welcome, gift item of some sort. It should, of course, be divisible if it is to be awarded to an enterprise which has more than one owner.

6. Ask participants to suggest which of the following motione for most successful businesswomen:

   ○ to make money

   ○ to complete the task they have set themselves according to their own standards

   ○ to do better than other people

   ○ to be independent

   Ensure that most participants have given their views, and then stress that it has generally been found that money and doing better than other people are *not* the main motives for businesswomen to succeed. They usually start a business because they wish to be independent and to judge their success themselves, rather than being judged by family, colleagues, teachers or others. Once they are involved they are motivated by the desire to achieve objectives they have set for themselves, not by the desire to earn more money or to be acknowledged as a great success by other people.

   Ask participants to examine their own motives, both within the Enterprise Experience and their real enterprises, if they are already in business. Why did they go into business themselves? If it was because they wanted to earn more money, is this really the most profitable option, has The Enterprise Experience heightened their awareness of the pleasure to be gained by succeeding, alone or with a team, in achieving objectives they have set for themselves?

7. If the participants in the course are trainers or others promoting small business, ask them whether this experience has changed their understanding of small businesspeople and their needs. In which way? How will this affect their own work in their organization back home?

Guidelines For The Presentation of The Final Results

1. Prepare a Profit and Loss Statement and calculate the profit or loss made per member of your business.

2. Prepare a Balance Sheet at the start of the business.

3. Prepare a Final Balance Sheet.

4. Prepare a flip-chart or overhead sheets for the session giving the following information:

   a. Name of the enterprise
   b. Name of the owner(s)
   c. The Profit and Loss Statement
   d. The profit or loss made and wages paid per member
   e. The Balance Sheet at start of the business
   f. The Final Balance Sheet.

5. Select a member of your team to present the final results. She will have a maximum of ten minutes for the presentation.

6. For those businesses which received a loan and have not yet repaid it: be prepared to repay it, including interest, at the beginning of the session.

7. Have your

   ○ cash book

   ○ records or accounts receivable and payable

   ○ any other records you have kept

   ○ and all the above information

   ready for the nominated time on the day before the final presentation.

Introduction to the Business Plan

PREPARATION   *Prepare one copy of the Planning Workbook for each participant.*

DURATION   *90 minutes*

SESSION GUIDE

1. The objective of this session is to enable participants to prepare a business plan and to realize its importance as a tool for planning the future of their businesses.

2. If the Enterprise Experience is part of your course: Remind participants of their Enterprise Experience businesses. Ask those who are not satisfied with their final results why they think they were not successful. Compare the figures given in their Enterprise Experience proposals with the actual results. Why are there such discrepancies in some cases? Elicit the suggestion that they used the 'Hit or Miss' approach instead of a careful planning of their business activities.

   Remind participants of the session 'Business Plan Preparation' of the Enterprise Experience where they suggested that a Business Plan has many purposes, such as:

   ○ it is the basis of a proposal for a loan to be presented to a bank or financing institution

   ○ it is a way of showing any outsider that the owner has thought seriously about her business and where it is going, and has assessed the future requirements in terms of cash, labour, materials and so on

   ○ and (most important) it is a working business tool, which enables a business owner to plan the future of her enterprise.

   If the Enterprise Experience is not part of this course, use steps 1 to 4 of the Business Plan Preparation (Session 3 of the Enterprise Experience to introduce the Planning Workbook, instead of steps 1 and 2 of this session guide.

3. Distribute the Planning Workbook. Explain that this is the basis for their forth-coming field work. They should use this workbook as a working document, to take notes and to work out preliminary figures. At the end of this course, after they have gathered all the necessary information, they will receive a new copy of this workbook and they will then have some time to prepare a business plan in such a way that they can make a presentation to a committee of bankers. The committee of bankers will be invited for the last day of this course, to give the participants feedback on how a banker judges the feasibility of the proposed businesses, and on the chances of getting a loan to start or expand the business.

4. Go through each question of the Planning Workbook. Show how the questions

relate both to completely new businesses, and to those which are already operating. Ensure by asking appropriate participants that all understand how each question should be answered.

Some participants may already own one business but plan to start another new one. Ensure that they make this clear in their Planning Workbook, and that information about separate businesses is not mixed up in their answers.

5. At the end of the session, point out again that each participant will be given a new copy of the Planning Workbook after the business investigation period, for completion and presentation to the Bankers' Panel, so they can, and should, use their first copies as working check-lists and field-guides.

The Planning Workbook

OWNER(S) NAME:

ADDRESS:

NAME OF BUSINESS:

DATE:

THE BUSINESS AND THE PEOPLE, TODAY AND IN THE FUTURE

1. Name and activity of the proposed business:

2. Name(s), age(s) and address(es) of owner(s), and their present occupations:

3. Summary of educational qualifications of owner(s):

4. Summary of previous employment or self-employment of owner(s), including those aspects which are relevant to the proposed business:

5. Brief statement of why owner(s) is/are particularly qualified to run this business:

6. (If more than one owner) What will each owner *do* in the business:

7. (If applicable) Brief description of the present operations of the business; location, products, sales, profit last year, number of employees:

8. (If applicable) Name(s) and brief description of other business(es) owned by the owner(s) of the business presented here:

9. The most important achievement of the business so far; or brief description of what the owner(s) have done so far towards starting the business:

10. The most important problem now facing the business, or likely to be faced when it starts:

THE MARKET

11. The present/proposed customers of the business (major customers such as other businesses and institutions by name, and, for individuals, their typical occupations, their location and approximate average income level):

12. The important competitors of the business, their numbers, locations, their apparent level of success, their weaknesses which this business proposes to improve upon:

13. Why do/will your customers buy from this business rather than from its competitors; its 'Unique Selling Point':

14. Additional customer information needed:

15. This information will be obtained as follows, including cost of any market survey, how long it will take, and any assistance needed:

THE MARKETING MIX

16. Prices to be charged are as follows (if there are many different items, or work is all specially made to individual order, give an indication of average price levels, and comparison with competition):

17. Reasons for choice of this general level of prices:

18. Advertising and promotion methods to be used, and approximate monthly cost:

19. Main message to be communicated by above promotion:

20. Main retail and/or wholesale distribution channels to be used, by name if possible, together with some indication of the gross profit margins they demand:

21. Reasons for choice of the above channel(s) of distribution:

22. Transport method(s) to be used for distribution, with approximate costs:

THE BUSINESS OPERATIONS

23. Main raw materials required, approximate present prices, named suppliers, and supply position (readily available, unreliable supplies etc.):

24. Transport proposed for above raw materials, with approximate costs:

25. Major existing items of equipment, with approximate age and value:

26. Major new equipment required, proposed sources of supply, approximate costs and delivery time (attach details, quotations):

27. Draw a very simple sketch of the existing/proposed layout, showing where stocks will be kept, and how work/goods will move from one process to another (Note: this applies as much to a business located at home as to one in a factory, and to an office or shop as to a manufacturing or processing business):

28. Proposed maintenance arrangements and costs:

29. Existing or proposed location of business, owned or rented; if rented, monthly rent:

30. Existing/proposed staff numbers, jobs and approximate monthly wages:

31. Proposed date(s) of hiring above new staff:

32. Any training required for above existing or proposed staff, or for owner(s) and its duration and cost:

33. Existing and proposed insurance, and approximate annual premiums:

34. Existing or proposed legal form of business:

35. Existing and future licences required, costs and where and how (to be) obtained:

THE RECORDS AND CONTROLS

36. What figures will you need to have about your business and how often:

37. Business records to be kept and who is/will be responsible for maintaining them:

FORECAST OF RESULTS AND FINANCIAL NEEDS

38. Estimated monthly sales, for next twelve months of operation (starting next month if already operating):

Starting month . . . . . . 19 . .

Month 1 . . . .   Month 4 . . . .   Month 7 . . . .   Month 10 . . . .

Month 2 . . . .   Month 5 . . . .   Month 8 . . . .   Month 11 . . . .

Month 3 . . . .   Month 6 . . . .   Month 9 . . . .   Month 12 . . . .

39. Total sales for the year: . . . .

40. Monthly costs for the same period:

a. Employees wages and salaries, not including owner: . . . .

b. Owner(s') salary: . . . .

c. Raw materials: . . . .

d. Transport: . . . .

e. Rent, electricity, fuel, other supplies not included in raw materials: . . . .

f. Other costs (specify): . . . .

g. Total of monthly costs: . . . .

41. Total annual costs (make appropriate changes for costs which will not be the same every month) . . . .

42. Annual profit or loss for above periods (39. less 41.) . . . .

43. Credit terms given to customers: . . . . days after delivery of goods

44. Credit terms received from raw material suppliers: . . . . days after delivery.

45. Payment date for any new equipment to be bought: . . . .

46. Forecast of cash flows in and out of business for first 12 months of operation (from next month if already in business) (Note: this should take account of credit terms etc. in items 43–45 above):

Months	1	2	3	4	5	6	7	8	9	10	11	12
CASH IN												
Balance												
Sales												
Other												
TOTAL IN												
CASH OUT												
Materials												
Wages												
Owner's Wage												
Equipment												
Rent												
Other												
TOTAL OUT												
BALANCE (+ or −)												

47. Maximum negative balance (if any): . . . .

and

Number of months in which business is negative: . . . .

48. (If negative balance has been shown above (in 47.) Revised cash flow forecast including loan and repayments:

Months	1	2	3	4	5	6	7	8	9	10	11	12
CASH IN												
Balance												
Loan												
Sales												
Other												
TOTAL IN												
CASH OUT												
Materials												
Wages												
Owner's Wage												
Equipment												
Rent												
Loan repay-ment.												
Other												
TOTAL OUT												
BALANCE (+ only)												

49. Loan required, if any (see 48.):. . . . .

50. Suggested repayment schedule:

First repayment: month . . . . 19 . .

Repayment per month . . . .

Final repayment: month . . . . 19 . .

51. Approximate balance sheet of business at start (start of next month, if already in business):

Date: . . . .

Sources of Money		Uses of money	
Owner's Capital	. . . .	Buildings	. . . .
Loans	. . . .	Vehicles	. . . .
Bank Overdraft	. . . .	Equipment	. . . .
Owed to Suppliers	. . . .	Owed by Customers	. . . .
Customer Deposits	. . . .	Bank Balance	. . . .
Other	. . . .	Cash	. . . .
		Other	. . . .
Totals	. . . .		. . . .

52. Estimated balance sheet 12 months from start date (12 months from now if already in business):

Date: . . . .

Sources of Money		Uses of money	
Owner's Capital	. . . .	Buildings	. . . .
Loans	. . . .	Vehicles	. . . .
Bank Overdraft	. . . .	Equipment	. . . .
Owed to Suppliers	. . . .	Owed by Customers	. . . .
Customer Deposits	. . . .	Bank Balance	. . . .
Other	. . . .	Cash	. . . .
		Other	. . . .
Totals	. . . .		. . . .

148

Preparation for business investigation

PREPARATION   *Prepare for this session by obtaining names, addresses and phone numbers (if applicable) of sources of information, such as libraries, business information centres, trade advisory centres and so on. If possible, borrow copies of useful directories; prepare a handout listing such sources.*

DURATION   *90 minutes*

This session should, if possible, follow immediately after the previous session 'Introduction to the Business Plan'.

SESSION GUIDE

1. Tell participants that the objective of this session is to enable them to obtain the information they need to work out a business plan for their enterprises, and to know how and where to get it.

2. During the following hour, participants will work in groups or individually: if several participants have similar business ideas, which are not likely to be in competition with one another, group them together. Participants whose businesses are unlike anyone else's should work individually.

   Allow these groups or individuals up to one hour to go through the Planning Workbook in detail on their own and to identify and write down items of information which they will need to obtain from outside sources, such as, for example, the cost of a sewing machine, the tailors in their neighbourhood (competitors) etc.

   Ask each group or individual to produce a list of such items of information.

3. Reconvene the groups. Display all the lists so as to have a basis for the following discussion.

   Encourage group discussion about problems participants may face, such as:

   ○ Competitors are not operating in their area.

   ○ Suppliers of equipment are located in the capital.

   ○ Proposed customers cannot imagine what the product will be like (how it will look or taste, and so on).

   ○ Competitors may be unwilling to share information.

   Elicit suggestions about how and where to get the required information, for example:

   ○ Approaching non-competitors in other places.

   ○ Telephoning or writing for information.

   ○ Using libraries or other public sources (if possible, distribute the prepared handout at this stage).

○ Pretending to be a student, or a potential customer rather than a possible competitor.

Remind participants of what they learned during the session 'Finding out about the market'. They should only search for useful, necessary information, and should use the Planning Workbook as a check-list.

NOTE: If possible, you and other resource people should be available for individual counselling after this session and during the business investigation period, and should be prepared for it, in that you and the other resource people know what kind of business each participant is planning and how and where to get useful information.

Report-back

PREPARATION   *None*

DURATION   *90 minutes*

SESSION GUIDE

1. The objective of this session is to enable participants to compare and discuss with others the information they obtained during their field study, and to identify topics which need revision.

2. Participants have now had a period for collecting as much information as possible to help them start or improve their businesses. Before going back home to do this investigation they received the Planning Workbook, and the prepared check-lists of information they had to obtain in order to complete the Workbook.

   During this session, participants can discuss their findings with their colleagues, and can together identify areas where they need further advice or training before they can successfully complete their Planning Workbooks.

3. Divide participants into several groups with the same or similar types of businesses. They should go through their findings and their Planning Workbooks, and compare their information, such as prices of raw materials, suppliers, and transport; it may be possible for participants to correct their findings, or to fill gaps, through discussion with other participants.

   Each group should also make a list of unclear issues (unclear questions in the Planning Workbook, uncertainty about how to work out certain figures, and so on), and be ready to share this with the other groups.

4. Reconvene the groups and ask their representatives each to present their lists of unclear issues.

   If necessary, additional evening sessions should be organized to repeat some of the important subjects like cash-flow, or costing and pricing, with which participants may still have difficulties, or it may be appropriate to arrange for smaller groups, or individuals, to receive advice and assistance with particular topics. Be sure to make use of participants themselves for this purpose; remind them of the initial session when they identified their strengths and weaknesses, and stress that the next few days when they will be completing their Planning Workbooks provide an ideal opportunity for sharing knowledge and helping one another.

The impact of your business

PREPARATION   *None*

DURATION   *135 minutes*

NOTE: The objective of this session is to enable participants to identify ways in which their businesses may damage the physical environment or may injure other people, and to identify ways by which such damage can be reduced or eliminated, and by which they can even profit from being socially and environmentally responsible.

It is important that participants should not be told the objective of the session at the beginning, as will be clear from the way it is structured. You should therefore either omit the usual statement of an objective, or say that the session is intended to enable participants to evaluate the longer term future of their businesses, in a general way.

SESSION GUIDE

1. Ask participants individually to 'dream' about the future of their businesses. If all goes well, and the plans in their Planning Workbooks are successfully implemented, in five years time about how many people will they be employing, what sort of share of the market will they have obtained, what volume of sales will they have achieved, around what quantities of what raw materials will they be using?

   They should not, at this stage, share their dreams with their colleagues, but should just allow their most optimistic thoughts free rein; the above questions are given to stimulate participants' imaginations, they need not come up with any more than very approximate orders of magnitude for numbers employed, sales and so on. They may make one or two brief notes for their own use if they wish to. Allow up to ten minutes for this 'dreaming' process.

2. Divide participants into groups of three to five members, and ask each member of each group briefly to describe her 'dream' to the other members; they may, if they wish, make brief notes for their own reference later in the session. Allow up to twenty minutes for this sharing stage of the session.

3. Now, and only now, when each member of each group has some idea of the possible future activities and scale of her fellow group members' businesses, ask the groups to attempt to identify at least one possible specific *negative* effect which each of the businesses might have, if and when it reached the scale and success of which its owner dreams.

   The negative effects might be:

   o on other people, by putting competitors out of business and causing unemployment o on the environment, by causing pollution, or destruction of forests

o on the economy, by increasing imports.

These are only examples, and participants should be encouraged to identify *specific* results which each business might have, which may fall into quite different categories from the above.

4. Allow up to forty-five minutes for this part of the session, and ensure, by observing and listening to the groups, that they understand what is required, and are avoiding generalizations. You should not make suggestions to them, but typical ill-effects might be:

   o A successful take-away restaurant might put needy women who are food vendors out of business, it might cause litter from discarded packaging and it might encourage children to eat 'junk food' rather than more nutritious and less expensive meals.

   o A successful rural baker might use large quantities of wood-fuel, she might displace locally-produced rice, maize or millet with imported wheat, and she might put local traditional food-processors out of business.

   o A successful ready-made clothing business might put local tailors out of business, it might replace local handloom cloth with mill-made material which requires less labour and it might displace traditional and culturally important local dress with 'modern' international styles.

5. Reconvene participants and ask a spokeswoman for each group to describe briefly the possible ill-effects which her group identified for each of its members' businesses.

   Summarize these on the board, and attempt to categorize them into groups such as those damaging the physical environment, those causing unemployment and those damaging the economy. Try to leave a space on the board beside each problem, for the purposes of the next stage as described below.

   Select a typical individual item from each of the categories, and ask the participant whose business might have this damaging effect to suggest ways in which she might minimize it, avoid it and even make more profit by treating the problem as an opportunity, which we earlier identified as being a characteristic of successful businesswomen.

   Summarize her suggestion on the board beside the statement of the problem, and invite alternative ideas and comments from others, particularly those whose businesses have been identified as possible causes of problems in the same category.

6. Identify a possible solution for at least one problem in each category, and for as many of the others as possible. Try to avoid giving the participants ideas yourself, but encourage them to be positive, if necessary by mentioning examples such as the following, which relate to the ill-effects listed above for a take-away, a bakery and a ready-made clothing business: these are all real-life examples, which have actually been successfully implemented by real businesses which were faced with these problems:

153

Take-away restaurant

○ Hire unemployed food vendors to provide a home delivery service.

○ Hire unemployed people to collect the business' and other rubbish, and sell it for recycling.

○ Develop and promote nutritious and relatively inexpensive children's snacks, as a profitable product in their own right and to encourage other sales.

Rural baker

○ Use alternative fuel sources, such as biogas or recycled waste, which may also become profitable businesses in their own right.

○ Offer attractive and less expensive breads made from wheat-flour blended with cassava (manioc) flour or other local products.

○ Develop local production of wheat, and local sustainable wood-fuel plantations.

○ Employ local people for delivering the bread to outlying areas.

Ready-made clothing

○ Employ local tailors and train them in factory production skills.

○ Use local tailors as 'outworkers' for specialized processes and items.

○ Design and promote more modern versions of traditional local dress, using local hand-woven cloth, for local, national and even export markets.

7. Not every suggestion will be practical, but encourage participants to take a positive view, and to recognize that the socially and environmentally responsible business decision is, in the long term, the 'right' decision not only for society in general but for the business itself and its owner(s).

Elicit a 'check-list' which participants can try to remember and to apply when making business decisions in the future.

This should include questions such as:

○ What effect will this have on employment, in my business and in other businesses which are affected by it?

○ How can I generate more jobs; by employing more people myself or by using other small businesses as suppliers or distributors of my products?

○ What effect will this have on the environment? Will it cause pollution, or will it damage natural resources?

○ How can I recycle damaging by-products or waste material; how can I develop local and sustainable material or fuel supplies?

○ What effect will this have on local producers of materials, or on the nation's import bill?

○ How can I make use of local materials; how can I develop improved local supplies so that I am less dependent on materials from elsewhere?

o What effect will this have on local culture, on eating habits, clothing or other traditional aspects of society which should be strengthened rather than destroyed?

o How can I develop good local traditions, recipes and designs in order to reinforce them and make them available to a wider market?

8. Prepare handouts of the 'check-list' you put together in step 7 and distribute them to the participants on the next possible occasion. The attached handout may serve as an example.

The Impact of Your Business on Society and The Environment

Every business has an effect on society and on the environment; decisions which appear to increase profits in the short-term may damage the business itself in the long-term, and we are all members of society and must depend on the wider environment. Businesswomen must be responsible, and it is often possible to make even short-term profits by treating possible social or environmental problems as business opportunities. Many very profitable new businesses are based entirely on environmental protection, recycling materials, developing sustainable sources of materials and so on.

Whenever you are making a business decision, you should consider its wider impact; the following check-list may help to identify possible damaging side-effects, and to identify potentially profitable ways of avoiding them:

Other people's jobs

○ What effect will this have on employment, in my business and in other businesses which are affected by it?

How can I generate more jobs; by employing more people myself or by using other small businesses as suppliers or distributors of my products?

The physical environment

○ What effect will this have on the environment? Will it cause pollution or will it damage natural resources?

How can I recycle damaging by-products or waste material; how can I develop local and sustainable material or fuel supplies?

The local and the national economy

○ What effect will this have on local producers of raw materials, or on the nation's import bill?

How can I make use of local materials; how can I develop improved local supplies so that I am less dependent on materials from elsewhere?

Health, culture and society

○ What effect will this have on local culture, on eating habits, clothing or other traditional aspects of society which should be strengthened rather than destroyed?

How can I develop good local traditions, recipes and designs in order to reinforce them and make them available to a wider market?

Completing the planning workbook

PREPARATION   *During the period assigned for the completion of the Plan-*
                 ning Workbooks, you and other advisers, if possible,
                 should be available for individual and small group coun-
                 selling and advice.

                 If possible, obtain copies of business loan application
                 forms used by local banks or other financial institutions.

                 Prepare a new copy of the Planning Workbook for each
                 participant.

DURATION   *60 minutes*

SESSION GUIDE

1. Tell participants that the objective of this session is to enable them to put all
   their business information and their forecasts and plans into one coherent
   document.

2. Be sure that participants understand that they have to complete their individual
   Planning Workbooks during the allotted period. Remind them of the deadline,
   that is the next full session on presentation skills, when some of them will be
   given the opportunity to practice the business presentations which they will all
   later be making to the bankers' panel.

   Some will protest that there is not enough time; remind them that working long
   hours and completing tasks according to customer deadlines are an important
   part of business success, and they should treat this assignment as an exercise for
   that purpose.

3. The following time allocation to the various sections of the Workbook may help
   participants to finish the Workbook within the given time; it is based on the
   assumption that three days have been allocated for the task and that the course is
   run on a full-time basis; equivalent periods should be allocated over a longer
   period if the course is a part-time one.

   o The Business and the People,
     Today and in the Future   half a day

   o The Market, The Business
     Operations   one day

   o The Records and Controls,
     Forecast of Results and
     Financial Needs   one and a half days

4. During the last day of this course participants will have to present their plans to a
   panel of bankers. The purpose of these presentations is to enable all participants
   to get feedback and advice from a group of people who are familiar with the

financial and other needs and problems of new and growing businesses. Those participants who have concluded that they need a loan will certainly not have their applications approved there and then, but the presentation, if it is convincing, may be the first step of a successful business loan application.

Remind particpants of the earlier session on Sources of Finance, and that there are many other faster, easier and less expensive ways of raising finance from within or outside a business which are available to many businesswomen. Some participants may discover from the business planning process that they do not need a loan; nobody should feel that she should ask for a loan just because she is presenting to a panel of bankers, and the presentation will be a valuable opportunity to benefit from expert advice and comments on their plans; bankers have an unrivalled knowledge of why businesses succeed and fail, and they usually welcome the opportunity to advise people who do not want a loan.

5. Point out that the completed Planning Workbook is *not* a complete Business Plan or loan application; it contains all the information ordinarily needed for a loan application, but it is not presented in the form which bankers usually expect.

Ask any participants who have any knowledge of loan applications how they would develop such an application from the Workbook; some banks have application forms, which can be filled in from the information in the Workbook, and if possible blank copies of such application forms should be given to interested participants at this time.

The following changes would normally be required to the layout and content of the Planning Workbook:

o The addition of an 'executive summary' at the beginning, stating, in half a page at most, the name and nature of the business, the owners' names, the sum required and the anticipated repayment period.

o Omission of the section numbers in the Workbook, and presentation of the content as statements rather than as answers to questions.

o A professionally-typed document, or at least a neat and attractively presented application which demonstrates a serious approach and a sense of high quality.

Participants who wish to apply for loans and are confident that they have all the necessary information may have time to 'convert' their Planning Workbooks into completed loan applications before meeting the bankers' panel. They should be encouraged to do this, provided that you are confident that they can make a convincing case, and it may even be possible for copies of such applications to be made available to members of the panel well before the presentation, particularly to any bankers who might actually be expected to make the loan.

Other participants may prefer to make their presentations from the Workbook, and to incorporate the panel members' comments and suggestions into their final applications. You should, if possible, advise and assist them in this process after the end of the course.

6. Distribute a new copy of the Planning Workbook for each participant, since they will need this to produce a final finished version before the panel presentations.

Practice business plan presentation

PREPARATION   *None*

DURATION   *180 minutes or more, depending on the time available; there should be between 15 and 20 minutes for each participant who is to practise her presentation.*

SESSION GUIDE

1. The objective of this session is to enable participants to improve their ability to present their business plans to bankers, and their presentation skills in general.

2. Remind participants of the strong and weak points of their Enterprise Experience presentations. Elicit guidelines for effective presentations, and list them on the board; they should include:

   o keeping to the allocated time

   o a clear sequence, with emphasis on the important issues

   o realistic and readily understandable figures

   o confident and persuasive self-presentation

   o clear, neat and precise visual aids, if they are used.

3. Ask as many participants as time allows to present their plans to the group; ensure that those who may be shy or uncertain are given a chance to have this opportunity to practise for the later presentation to bankers, as well as the more confident since they are more likely to need practice and advice.

4. Nominate a participant to act as the 'banker' for each practice presentation, allow ten minutes *only* for each presentation, invite comments, questions and advice from the other participants, and then ask the nominated 'banker' to comment on it under the following headings:

   o Was the presentation completed within the time given?

   o Was the sequence clear, with a beginning, a middle and an end?

   o Were all the important issues covered?

   o Were the figures realistic, and was the arithmetic correct?

   o Did the appearance and manner of the participant inspire confidence in her ability to manage a business and to deal with customers and suppliers?

   o Did her answers to her colleagues' questions suggest that she was totally familiar with the details of her business?

   o Would the 'banker' herself lend money to this business?

4. Elicit further comments and advice from the rest of the group before proceeding

to the next presentation, and ensure that as many participants as possible have this opportunity to practise their presentation skills, which are needed for selling, buying, for dealing with officials and with employees as well as presenting applications for finance.

How To Present Your Business Plan To Your Banker

1. Remember: Your potential source of finance will be impressed and more likely to lend a sympathetic ear to your business plan if you organize your facts well. Therefore, think through your presentation, argue your case clearly and be optimistic – remember that every bank manager is firmly on your side, after all she/he makes money by financially supporting business enterprise proposals like yours.

2. Put yourself in the bank manager's shoes. Would you lend money on the strength of your presentation? Bear in mind that the bank manager is trying to run a business at a profit too.

3. Do not just be optimistic. Your figures will not be taken on trust, so substantiate them as much as possible.

4. Do not leave it all to the last minute. Give yourself plenty of time to prepare your business plan and your presentation.

5. Completing the Planning Workbook may seem a huge task; it takes a great deal of work but once you start setting up on your own, you will find that all the pieces fit together much more easily than you would have thought.

6. The actual presentation is vitally important, because it gives the bankers an opportunity to judge you, as a person, and your personality is the most important determinant of the success of your business and thus of your ability to repay a loan.

   Make sure that you keep to the following guidelines:

   ○ Keep the presentation to the time given.

   ○ Follow a clear sequence, with a beginning, a middle and an end.

   ○ Cover all the important issues.

   ○ Make sure the figures are realistic, and the arithmetic is correct.

   ○ Your appearance and manner must inspire confidence in your ability to manage a business and to deal with customers and suppliers.

   ○ Your answers to the banker's questions must show that you are totally familiar with the details of your business.

Presentations to the bankers' panel

DURATION   *30 minutes per business (the presentations may be made to more than one panel if participant numbers require this, see below.)*

At least one month before this session, you should invite the panel members to participate. Each panel should ideally consist of three people, of whom one at least should be a commercial banker, one should be a representative of an appropriate small-business financing institution and the third might be another banker or financier, a representative of a business advisory service or a successful business owner. As many as possible of the panel members should be women, but it is more important that they should be people who actually have responsibility for approving loans of this type.

You must convince every participant, even those who may be very nervous, that she must make a presentation to the bankers' panel, because she will gain so much confidence from the experience. Participants should be provided, well in advance, with flip chart or newsprint sheets, or overhead projector transparencies for their visual aids, and individual guidance should be available to them during the preparation period. When two or more participants are involved in one business, they must clearly agree on what role each is to play in the presentation.

Each participant, or group of participants, should make a ten minute presentation, followed by twenty minutes for questions, comment and discussion, and there should therefore be more than one panel if this is necessary to accommodate all the participants in the period available for the presentations.

It is vital that the administrative arrangements should enhance the impact of the participants' presentations:

○ The timetable should be clearly printed and distributed in advance.

○ The panel members should be properly briefed on the purpose of the exercise.

○ The rooms should be properly laid out and equipped with available visual aids.

○ You should ensure that timings are maintained.

If possible, the presentations should be followed by a lunch or similar occasion, attended by all participants, trainers and the panel members, both to show appreciation of the panel members' efforts, and to give an opportunity for informal follow-up discussions with participants which often lead to eventual loan approvals.

Follow-up

The participants have now completed their training, but they are only just starting the hard and often lonely task of implementing what they have learned; many people become discouraged if the transition from the classroom to the real world is too sudden. They have been working for some time with a group of friends and with your encouragement; you must help them to re-enter the harsh, competitive world of business.

You should try to keep in touch with the participants in any case, in order to evaluate the course, as already discussed on pages 20 and 21, and to improve your own understanding of the problems and opportunities facing women in business. The types of follow-up that you can do will depend on where the women are and on the type of institution you work for, but you should at least be able to do some of the following:

○ Maintain regular contact by mail, perhaps circulating a quarterly newsletter.

○ Assist the women to form an association for mutual support.

○ Visit as many as possible of the women yourself, without making a nuisance of yourself.

○ Be ready to meet individual women, at home or in your office, when they need assistance and counselling.

○ Introduce women to banks, potential customers and other sources of support.

○ Assist women to overcome difficulties with the authorities.

○ Work closely with local business support agencies which provide extension services or other assistance.

○ Invite participants to a reunion workshop six months or so after the training, for the exchange of experiences and ideas.

The best form of encouragement is the example of other successful businesswomen. If you can help your ex-participants to succeed you will be indirectly helping many others whom you will never even meet to do the same, and thus to work towards a better life for themselves, their families, their communities and society as a whole.

Reading list

WOMEN IN BUSINESS

Buvinic, M. *et al., Women and Poverty in the Third World*, Baltimore, Johns Hopkins University Press, 1983.

Buvinic, M. and Youssef, M., *Women-headed households in the Third World countries: An overview*, Washington DC, ICRW, 1978.

Carr, M., *Blacksmith, Baker, Roofing-sheet maker; employment for rural women in developing countries*, London, IT Publications, 1984.

——. *Technology and rural women in Africa*, Geneva, ILO, 1980.

Clutterbuck, D. and Devine, M., *Businesswoman: Present and Future*, London, Macmillan, 1987.

Downing, J., *Gemini; Gender and the growth and dynamics of microenterprise*; report prepared for the Gemini-Project, US-AID; Washington, July 1990.

Dulansey, M. and Austin, J., 'Small-scale enterprise and women' in Overholt, C., Anderson, M.B., Cloud, K. and Austin, J., *Gender roles in development projects: A case book*, Connecticut, Kumarian Press, 1984.

El-Namaki, M.S.S. and Gerritson, J.C.M., 'The entrepreneurial role of women in developing countries: entry and performance barriers', *RVB Research Paper*, Vol. VII, No. 1, March 1987.

Goffee, R. and Scase, R., *Women in charge: the experience of female entrepreneurs*, London, George Allen and Unwin, 1985.

Hertz, L., *Business Amazons*, London, Deutsch, 1986.

Hisrich, R. D., 'The woman entrepreneur: Characteristics, skills, problems and perspectives of success', in Sexton, Donald L. and Smilor, Raymond W. (eds.) *The art and science of entrepreneurship*, Cambridge, Mass., 1986, pp. 61–85.

Hisrich, R. D. and Brush, C., *Woman entrepreneur: Starting, financing and managing a successful new business*, Toronto, Lexington Books, 1986.

Jumani, U., *Women in Business: Strengthening Women's Economic Activities*, Ahmedabad, Jumani Foundation, March 1991.

Kindervatter, S., *Women working together for personal, economic and community development*, Washington, Overseas Education Fund, 1983.

Sandler, J., Sandhu, R., (eds.), *The Tech and Tools Book: A guide to the technologies used by women around the world*, London, IT Publications, 1986.

Snyder, M., Women, the key to ending hunger, *The Hunger Project Papers*, No. 8, New York, August 1990.

Van Der Wees, C. and Romijn, H., Entrepreneurship and small enterprise development for women in developing countries: An agenda for unanswered questions (draft). Geneva, ILO, Management Development Branch, 1987.

TRAINING

Dickson, D.E.N. (ed.), *Improve Your Business Handbook. Improve your Business Workbook*; Geneva, ILO, 1986.

Harper, M., *Consultancy for Small Business*, London, IT Publications, 1977.

Harper, M., *Entrepreneurship for the Poor*, London, IT Publications, 1984.

Harper, M., *Small Business in the Third World. Guidelines for practical assistance*, London, J. Wiley & Sons/IT Publications, 1984.

Harper, M. and Vyakarnam, S., *Rural Enterprise: case studies from developing countries*, London, IT Publications, 1988.

Hurley, D. and Duke, S., *Income generation schemes for the urban poor*, Oxford, Oxfam, 1990.

Kelley, M. *et al., Doing a feasibility study – training activities for third world women entrepreneurs*, Washington D.C. OEF International, 1986.

Kindervatter, S. *et al., Marketing strategies – training activities for third world women entrepreneurs*, Washington D.C., OEF International, 1986.

Millard, E., *Financial Management of a Small Handicraft Business*, London, IT Publications/Oxfam, 1987.

Van den Bogaert, M., *Training village entrepreneurs: guidelines for development workers*, Skills for Progress, 1986.

Many of the books listed here can be obtained from IT Publications, London.